# What Others Are
# Saying

Pastor Realton and I have come a long way together in our journey as youth in the same ministry for almost a decade. In this book, the man of God has expounded on many secrets and given a clear description of what the child of God possesses and what is at our disposal through the Word and our words. This book is loaded with revelation—not only on the revelation of God's name as our banner and protector—but it also provides a step-by-step guide on how to access the full extent of God's provision daily.

I was challenged as a minister of the gospel not only to store more of the Word in me but to keep the Word constantly in my mouth. Also, the very thought that the Lord does not leave us without His protection was so comforting and reassuring of His love.

Dig into this book, have a notepad while reading it, and make marks and notes in your Bible. It is truly a complete spiritual meal and a tool God will use to help you grow and become more aware of His protection.

– Apostle Winston Mashigo
Senior Pastor, Championship Ministries
South Africa

This book has given me a deeper appreciation for divine protection. As believers, we can live under God's banner of protection if we understand the battle and know how to declare the Word of God for our protection. It is scripture-rich, anchored in the belief that God is our ultimate refuge and shield. When you read through this book, you will develop confidence in God's protection for all areas of your life.

It is very relevant—especially living in a country where your security and safety are always threatened. I haven't come across literature with such comprehensive insights on God's protection. *Yahweh Nissi* should be read by every believer in South Africa.

– **Reagan Mitchell**
**CEO, WealthyMe**
**South Africa**

---

This is a very insightful book, delving deeply into the often-underestimated power of the spoken word, and revealing its profound impact on our inner world and external reality. Through compelling anecdotes and practical guidance, Realton illuminates how our language shapes our thoughts, beliefs, and ultimately, our experiences. It serves as a potent reminder that the words we choose carry immense energy—capable of both building and destroying.

By encouraging mindful communication and the conscious use of positive affirmations, Realton empowers readers to harness the transformative potential of speaking the Word of God over any situation, with the goal of cultivating a more intentional and fulfilling life. It is a concise yet powerful read for anyone seeking to understand and wield the subtle yet significant force backing us when we put the Word of God into our daily communication. I can see your life turning around and heading in the right direction as you read this book.

– **Apostle Shammah Apwam**
**Senior Pastor, Greater Glory Tabernacle**
**& Remnant Glory Network**
**Madagascar**

---

Realton Suliman is a powerful voice in practical, faith-filled living. Realton has such a gift for making scripture deeply personal and incredibly practical. YAHWEH NISSI is more than a book—it's a spiritual toolkit for anyone seeking to live under God's divine covering. With sections like "Declaring the Word," "Understanding the Battle," and "Living Under the Banner," each chapter guides readers into a deeper revelation of God's covenant of protection. From angelic interventions to practical tools for spiritual warfare, this book will transform the way you approach daily life. If you've ever wondered how to apply scripture in times of uncertainty, fear, or spiritual attack—YAHWEH NISSI is your answer.

– **Darren August**
**CEO, Inspired Publishing**
**South Africa**

# YAWHEH NISSI

# REALTON SULIMAN

# YAWHEH NISSI

**SUPERNATURAL** SAFETY
& **PROTECTION** IS YOURS!

INSPIRED PUBLISHING

**Yahweh Nissi**

Supernatural Safety and Protection Is Yours!

First Edition, First Imprint 2025

ISBN: 978-1-0370-7940-5

Copyright © Realton Suliman

Editor: Eloise Scoble

Published by: Inspired Publishing
PO Box 82058 | Southdale | 2135 Johannesburg, South Africa
Email: info@inspiredpublishing.co.za
www.inspiredpublishing.co.za

# TABLE OF CONENTS

# ACKNOWLEDGEMENTS

Wonderful Jesus, I lift my heart in gratitude for Your loving grace that has made this journey possible. From the very first thought to the final word, You have been with me every step of the way, guiding me through the precious counsel of Your Holy Spirit. This book is the fruit of prayer, fasting, and deep study, and I give You all the glory for granting me the strength, wisdom, and endurance to bring it to completion. I will forever be grateful for Your divine help and unwavering presence.

To my precious mother, Abiba, thank you for your unconditional love, support, and prayers. Your strength and faith have been a source of inspiration, and I honour you for everything you have instilled in me. To my wonderful late grandmother, Kadija, I cherish the principles of respect, integrity, humility, and kindness that you taught me. Your love, guidance, and prayers have shaped me into the God-fearing man I am today. Until we meet again, Ouma, I will carry your legacy with love and honour.

To my siblings, Joshua and Cordelia, thank you for your love and unwavering support. Your encouragement has meant the world to me, and I am truly blessed to walk this journey with you by my side.

I also extend my deepest appreciation to my spiritual parents, Apostle Shammah and Prophetess Patricia Apwam, for your love, prayers, and support. Your covering and encouragement have been invaluable, and I thank God for your presence in my life.

To my beloved family—my wonderful wife, Rosslyn, and our amazing children, Haggai, Nehemiah, Elijah, and Hadassah— words cannot express the depth of my gratitude. Thank you for your love, patience, and prayers, for standing by me as I dedicated countless hours to writing and seeking the Lord in the early hours of the morning. I know it took much from our family time, but your sacrifices, understanding, and unwavering support have made this possible. I love and appreciate you immensely.

Lastly, to all the incredible men of God who took the time to review, endorse, and support this book, I am deeply grateful. May the Lord continue to bless, enlarge, and reward you abundantly for your kindness and encouragement.

Much love and appreciation to you all.

# DEDICATION

This book is lovingly dedicated to every heart that has known the grip of fear, the weight of anxiety, and the silent ache of despondency—to those who have tossed and turned in the stillness of night, wrestling with the uncertainty of what tomorrow may bring. It is for the many souls in our beloved South Africa and beyond, who wake each day burdened by the reality of crime, violence, and the constant threat to their safety.

This book is also for those who, in a fleeting moment of crisis, have found themselves overwhelmed and momentarily lost sight of their identity in Jesus Christ—for those who have questioned if they are truly covered, if they are truly seen, and if they are truly safe in His hands. If you have ever felt that fear has stolen your peace, if the shadows of doubt have crept into your mind, this book is a beacon of light and a gentle reminder that you are never alone.

You are not forgotten. You are not without refuge. You are deeply loved, fiercely protected, and eternally held by the One who never sleeps nor slumbers. May the words within these pages renew your confidence in Him, strengthen your faith, and restore your hope in His unfailing promises. May you come to know, with unwavering certainty, that Yahweh Nissi, the Lord our Banner, is forever your shield and shelter.

Psalm 32:7<sup>(NIV)</sup>
*"You are my hiding place; You will protect me from trouble and surround me with songs of deliverance."*

With all my heart, I dedicate this book to you.

# DISCLAIMER

I know that there are those who do not believe in "decreeing and declaring", because it is often associated with the Prosperity Gospel or Word of Faith movement, which teaches that believers can speak things into existence or claim material blessings through faith-filled declarations. They argue that this theology can lead to a focus on personal gain rather than God's glory and can distort the biblical understanding of faith, suffering, and God's sovereignty. However, what I am teaching is not a "name it, claim it" system. I believe that we do have the authority to decree and declare, when we are tapping into what heaven has already said, and we are appropriating it for ourselves, our families, churches, communities and even the world, in the time and realm we are living in. Everything that we declare needs to match up to scripture, and to the Rhema word God has placed in you for the situation that you are encountering.

# VARIOUS BIBLE VERSIONS USED IN THIS BOOK

The following Bible translations were used throughout this manuscript. Scripture quotations are cited using their respective abbreviations. These translations were chosen to bring clarity, depth, and faith-based insight to the teaching and prophetic declarations presented in this book:

1. **NIV**
   New International Version Bible. (2011). Zondervan.

2. **NRSV**
   New Revised Standard Version Bible. (1989). Division of Christian Education of the National Council of the Churches of Christ in the United States of America.

3. **ESV**
   English Standard Version Bible. (2001). Crossway Bibles.

4. **BSV**
   Berean Standard Bible. (2020). Bible Hub.
   https://berean.bible

5. **NKJV**
   New King James Version Bible. (1982). Thomas Nelson.

6. **KJV**
   King James Bible. (1769/1987). Thomas Nelson.

7. **ERV**
   Easy-to-Read Version Bible. (2006). World Bible Translation Center.

## Referencing Format

All commentaries and source materials cited throughout this book are numbered in the order they appear and correspond to the full **Reference Index** at the back of the book. This format has been intentionally chosen to ensure clarity and accessibility, allowing readers to easily locate the source of each citation while engaging with the content.

# PROLOGUE

There is a gripping song by South African gospel artist, Ntokozo Mbambo, that many of us may be familiar with. Its lyrics are simple, but profound, and its sweet melody is as soothing and comforting, as it is authoritative.

The song *"Jehovah is your name"*[1] resonates through its repeated refrain:

> *"Jehovah is Your Name*
> *Jehovah is Your Name*
> *Jehovah is Your Name*
> *Jehovah is Your Name*
>
> *Mighty warrior*
> *Great in battle*
> *Jehovah is Your Name"*

If you have not encountered it before or are not yet familiar with it, I invite you to seek it out and listen, allowing yourself to be enveloped and immersed in the comforting presence of God. I assure you that it will set the tone and create the perfect stage for our journey ahead. And if you already know it as well as I do, then you understand that we are preparing to enter a most holy and sacred space, where we can become more intimately acquainted with an all-powerful God.

Our God, the one we call Jehovah, is known by many names.

Jehovah is a Latinised form of the Hebrew name Yahweh, and there exist numerous names that incorporate Jehovah.

The name Yahweh is the most personal designation that God gives Himself in the Old Testament, and when it is paired with other descriptive terms, it becomes a unique identifier of His character.

For instance, when we say Jehovah Jireh, we are declaring that *"The Lord Will Provide";* with Jehovah Shalom, we affirm that *"The Lord is Peace";* through Jehovah Rapha, we acknowledge *"The Lord That Heals";* with Jehovah Tsidkenu, we proclaim *"The Lord Our Righteousness";* and by calling Him Jehovah Raah, we recognise *"The Lord My Shepherd."*

These names are far more than mere titles or labels; they are a true reflection of God's nature and character. By studying the various names of God and their meanings in the Bible, we gain profound insights into who He is and how He relates to us.

Come with me as we delve into Jehovah Nissi – *"The Lord My Banner."*

Linda Smallwood, in her study of this sacred name on myredeemerlives.com[2], explains that the term "nissi" is derived from the Hebrew "nês," meaning "banner" or "to flee for refuge."

It is sometimes translated as "standard," referring to a pole adorned with an insignia. In ancient warfare, nations would raise their standards at the front lines to inspire hope and provide a clear focal point for their soldiers.

By uniting God's personal name with this descriptive term, we arrive at "YHWH Is My Banner" or "YHWH Is My Refuge." This compound name encapsulates the role of God as a constant beacon of encouragement and hope. As Smallwood further notes, in the context of ancient battle, a banner was not merely a symbol but a vital point of focus for the soldiers, reminding them that even in the midst of adversity, God remains a steadfast emblem of encouragement and protection.

Smallwood goes on to explain that, in addition to the compound name's single appearance in Exodus 17:15, the individual word "nissi," meaning "banner," appears in several other passages.

In Psalm 60:4[NKJV] the scripture declares, *"You have given a banner *[nissi] to those who fear You, that it may be displayed because of the truth. Selah,"* while in Song of Solomon 2:4 we read, *"He brought me to the banquet hall. His banner *[nissi] over me is love."* *Added for emphasis

The prophet Isaiah also employs this term on multiple occasions: in Isaiah 5:26[NKJV] it is written[3], *"He will lift up a banner [nissi] to the nations from far, and He will whistle for them from the end of the earth. Behold, they will come speedily and swiftly,"* and Isaiah 31:9 notes, *"And he shall pass over to his stronghold for fear, and his rulers shall be afraid of the banner [nissi],"* while Isaiah 49:22 states, *"Thus says the Lord Yahweh, 'Behold, I will lift up my*

*hand to the nations, and set up my ensign [nissi] to the peoples;*
*and they shall bring your sons in their bosom, and your daughters*
*shall be carried on their shoulders.'"*

These references, drawn from the World English Bible, further
enrich our understanding of "nissi" as not only a symbol of divine
guidance but also as a sign of hope and protection.

# PART 1

# DECLARING THE WORD

This opening section lays the foundation for everything that follows. In these chapters, you will discover the incredible power of the spoken Word of God. Supernatural safety begins with your voice—when it echoes heaven, it releases authority on earth. You will be equipped to speak God's promises boldly, align your declarations with Scripture, and use your words as weapons against fear, confusion, and danger. As you move through these pages, prepare to activate your faith and shift the spiritual atmosphere around you. Yahweh Nissi, your banner, goes before you—and your words make way for His covering.

# 1

# THE FOUNDATION OF DIVINE PROTECTION

Understanding the Times and The Need for Protection

---

Every generation brings its own set of challenges and evils that we must face. Today's world seems to be filled with dangers that are more real than ever before. The daily reality of leaving home and never returning, or being at home only to be robbed, experiencing a car accident, falling victim to hijacking, or even being struck by a stray bullet has never felt so immediate in the history of mankind. We are constantly reminded of these threats, as news reports reveal carjackings, smash and grabs, abductions, and the grim possibility of being hurt or killed at any moment.

Every corner of our world now seems shrouded in fear and hopelessness, as darkness appears to cover the earth. In South

Africa, it has become frightening to simply live a normal life. Whether we are going to work to provide for our families, taking our children to school, visiting loved ones, shopping, going on holiday, or even enjoying a casual walk or jog, there is always the worry that we might be the next victim of crime. Safety has become a major concern for all South Africans, regardless of ethnicity, skin colour, or economic status, and indeed, this is not just a South African problem—it is a global issue affecting all of mankind.

In recent years, various news channels have reported tragic incidents where children, teachers, and security personnel have been killed in places once thought to be safe, such as schools. Despite the many safety precautions that we adopt or consider, we still never feel secure because the threat of harm, injury, or death is ever-present. The SAPS Annual Crime Report of 2019[4], reported that fifty-eight people are murdered every day at a rate of 36.4 murders per 100,000 people, based on the latest population estimates. This figure does not even include other serious crimes like sexual offences, carjacking, burglary, kidnapping, or child trafficking, painting a bleak picture of our daily reality in South Africa.

It is on this foundation of fear and insecurity that the inspiration for this book was born, not only because of these unsettling statistics but also due to the personal tragedy of my brother, who was nearly killed by a stray bullet. With all the government interventions—both effective and lacking—it becomes clear that true safety and protection can only come from God. No matter what one believes, real safety, peace, and protection can only be experienced through the Lord Jesus Christ.

This book continues the teaching centred on my previous book - "The Spoken Word" - a concept that highlights the importance of faith declarations based on scripture to bring about change in our lives, communities, and the world.

However, our focus here is specifically on **Supernatural Safety and Protection.** We will speak our faith concerning God's promises of safety and divine protection, and we will pray and embrace the complete work that Christ Jesus achieved through His supernatural resurrection, standing firm against the forces of darkness.

The bible states, *"For the word of God is quick, and powerful, and sharper than any two-edged sword, piercing even to the dividing asunder of soul and spirit, and of the joints and marrow, and is a discerner of the thoughts and intents of the heart." Hebrews 4:12*[NIV]

This passage is truly remarkable. In this passage, the *Word of God* is described as "quick". The Greek word "ζάω" (zaó)[5] means "to live, to be alive, living, lively".

*The Greek word "δύναμις" (dunamis)[6] means "power, strength, ability, might, miracle".* This emphasizes that God's word is not static or passive, but dynamic and impactful.

"Sharper" than any double-edged sword, possessing an edge capable of cutting deeply. This imagery highlights the penetrating nature of God's word, capable of cutting through the deepest parts of a person's being.

Such language tells us that this living and dynamic word is not to be taken lightly. Its supernatural in nature, able to divide soul and spirit, even reaching down to the very joints and marrow, and it discerns the innermost intentions of the human heart.

It is no wonder that when we come into direct contact with the forces of darkness and declare the Word of God by faith, something supernatural happens. The enemy and the kingdom of darkness detest these deliberate and intentional declarations of the Word, because it penetrates through every form of resistance, every evil operation and any atmospheres that stands in opposition to the Word and the kingdom of God. This powerful proclamation disrupts their evil arrangements, causing confusion and unseating thrones of wickedness. I have witnessed occasions during ministry, under the power of the Spirit of God, where those very forces— devils that conspire against the destinies of people, communities and nations —become so agitated and angry that they manifest in unusual ways. When the Word, which is the logos (written Word), becomes the rhema or the spoken word, it exposes their operations and renders them null and void. In declaring the word by faith, these dark forces lose their power to achieve their evil agendas.

The continuous, deliberate and intentional prophetic declarations of the Word concerning our wellbeing has the power to create new realities and atmospheres in which miracles can manifest in our lives, our community and our world. Demons despise the Word and will do everything in their power to prevent us from coming to the revelation, and understanding of the power that is locked within these prophetic declarations. Just imagine what would happen if the entire world united in declaring and speaking the

Word consistently, deliberately and daily. Our communities, families and the world at large would be transformed into a very different place.

Isaiah 55:10-11 [NIV]

*"As the rain and the snow come down from heaven, and do not return to it without watering the earth and making it bud and flourish, so that it yields seed for the sower and bread for the eater, so is my word that goes out from my mouth: It will not return to me empty, but will accomplish what I desire and achieve the purpose for which I sent it."*

The Word of God is as natural and life-giving as the rain and snow that nourish the earth. It follows a fundamental pattern: when the right conditions are present, germination must occur and growth inevitably follows. Just as the elements from heaven fall to water the soil, prompting seeds to sprout and flourish, so too does God's word take root in our lives. It instigates a process of transformation and renewal, fostering the change our hearts so earnestly seek. This divine promise of growth and restoration is as certain as the natural cycle of the seasons.

## 2

# THE POWER OF THE TONGUE

Speaking Life or Death

---

Our words hold immense power—more than we often realise. The Bible makes it clear that life and death are in the power of the tongue, and what we choose to speak will shape our reality. Whether we bless or curse, build or destroy, our words carry weight in both the physical and spiritual realms.

In this chapter, we will explore the profound impact of spoken words, the authority behind them, and how they shape our destinies. As we uncover biblical truths, we will gain insight into how to harness the power of our tongues to speak life, activate divine blessings, and align ourselves with God's will.

Proverbs 18:21[(NIV)] *states: "The tongue has the power of life and death, and those who love it will eat its fruit."*

Have you ever wondered why God's Word is described as the snow and the rain, while our words—the expressions that come from our tongues—are described as the resulting fruit? When we look at the passage from Isaiah 55:10-11, we see that God's word will always accomplish what it has been sent out to do.

Unlike so many things in life, God's Word has a 100% success rate —there is no failure, no fault, and no delay in its effect. It is as certain as the cycle of precipitation we all learned about as children.

Just as rain and snow fall, nurture the soil, and cause seeds to sprout without any pause, so too does God's word bring about the change and results it promises *every single time.* This divine process is automatic and perfect, establishing a direct connection between the spoken word of God and the life-giving outcomes it produces.

We know there is no delay because it is compared to the natural cycle of precipitation we studied as children, and in that there is no delay. Typically, we learn that this cycle begins when the sun heats water in rivers, lakes, and oceans, causing it to evaporate into invisible water vapour that rises into the sky. As the water vapour reaches cooler air at higher altitudes, it condenses into tiny droplets to form clouds. When these droplets gather and become heavy, they fall back to the Earth as rain, snow, or other forms of precipitation. Once the water reaches the ground, it collects in streams, rivers, and lakes, and the entire process starts afresh.

While we are often taught that this cycle involves water moving from the Earth to the sky and back again, the scripture hints that it actually begins in the sky. It begins with God, with the Word of

God. God's Word originates from heaven and unfailingly produces the fruit of life and transformation.

So, you may be asking yourself: why then has it "failed" for me? Many of us have asked of God, from the Word of God, using the Word of God, only to feel that our requests are denied.

The answer is that, while our words are like seeds, they need the right conditions to yield their fruit. Just as the earth requires proper nourishment to transform a seed into a flourishing plant, our words too, when used with care and wisdom, can bring forth life and healing. Conversely, careless words can create conditions that lead to destruction and despair.

Our words have the potential to be used for either good or evil, and the fruit they bear will inevitably reflect their usage. It is therefore essential to recognise the immense power of our tongues, as they possess the ability to shape the course of our lives, our families, our communities, and even our nation.

James 3:8-10[NKJV] reiterates this point *"But the tongue can no man tame; it is an unruly evil, full of deadly poison. Therewith bless we God, even the Father; and therewith curse we men, which are made after the similitude of God Out of the same mouth proceed blessing and cursing..."*

Most of us take it for granted what it is to bless and to what it is to curse. Pronouncing a blessing involves invoking a higher power or deity to bestow the proclaimed blessings. Blessings in the biblical context were often spoken by patriarchs, priests, and prophets – men who had leverage in the heavenlies; who had a certain amount of authority given to them by God.

33

Similarly, pronouncing a curse involves calling upon a supernatural or divine power to inflict harm or misfortune on a specific person or entity.

The difference between these two is the authority it falls under. Our words, both good and bad fall under a specified authority, and one who assigns that these words (or assignments) be carried out.

Our speech can effectively authorise actions; it can either grant the devil a legal right to bring about destruction or empower the Kingdom of God to usher in life and blessings.

Another way to understand the quoted proverb, "*death and life are in the power of the tongue*" is to say that we live or die by our words.

Verse 20 of the same chapter underscores this truth by stating, *"A man's belly shall be satisfied with the fruit of his mouth; and with the increase of his lips shall he be filled."* This serves as a potent reminder that we must not take our words lightly. The things we say have lasting consequences, and many of us may find ourselves suffering the repercussions of thoughtless remarks made in the past. Each word carries the potential to build up or break down, to inspire hope or to foster despair. It is a call to be deliberate and mindful in our speech, understanding that every utterance holds the power to transform our lives and the lives of those around us.

Proverbs 6:2[(NKJV)] states, "*You are snared by the words of your mouth; you are taken by the words of your mouth*". While it essentially warns against being trapped by our own promises or agreements, we need to understand that every word we utter is an agreement with a force we do not see or often consider.

Matthew 12:36 warns us that we will be *"held accountable for every idle word."* This solemn caution makes it clear that on the day of judgement, each careless word we have spoken will be scrutinised. It is important to note that, in the context of this scripture, an "idle word" refers to words spoken thoughtlessly, casually, or without meaningful purpose, rather than necessarily those that are malicious in nature.

This emphasises the profound importance of our words. When we realise that, in the spiritual realm, there is no such thing as mere entertainment, we understand that every word, every action, and every thought carries a distinct intent and purpose. Even when we engage in what we consider to be light-hearted banter or casual conversation, we are, perhaps unknowingly, sending out assignments into the spiritual domain. Our seemingly trivial words can dispatch entities and set in motion consequences without our full awareness of their true impact.

Negative words serve as access points for the devil, allowing demonic influences to enter our lives. These destructive forces can manipulate circumstances and alter our destinies, all with the sole aim of causing harm, stealing, and destroying.

The potential and power of our tongues are limitless, which is why it is crucial to be mindful of every word we speak. Our words *literally* have the ability to bring about either death or life, in any and every situation.

While we may often regard this as mere figurative language, the truth is that the way a matter unfolds—whether it moves closer to life or towards death—depends entirely on the words we speak about it, around it, and concerning it.

In this context, death does not refer to an immediate, sudden occurrence as soon as negative words are uttered; rather, it signifies a gradual death by decay. It is like speaking a cancer into a situation, where each negative word compounds the effect, making the situation increasingly unwell. This slow poison gradually erodes life, health, longevity, and ultimately, the success of any endeavour.

Like a small fire that can quickly spread and devastate entire areas, our spoken words can ignite situations that affect not only our lives but also those of others around us.

**3**

# THE RIGHT CONDITIONS

Aligning Words with Divine Authority

---

The words we speak have the power to shape our reality, but without the right conditions, they remain ineffective. When we declare God's Word, we align our speech with divine authority, setting in motion the supernatural forces that bring His promises to fulfillment.

This chapter explores the importance of speaking in agreement with heaven, ensuring that our declarations are not based on personal desires but on the unshakable truth of God's Word. By understanding the spiritual laws that govern our words, we can activate divine intervention, break strongholds, and see tangible results in our lives.

When we speak according to God's word, we are making a declaration, or setting forth a decree. We are in essence, exercising our dominion authority and activating the power of the Holy Spirit dwelling within us. This empowers us to command change and effect significant impact, as expressed in Job 22:28[AMP]: "*You will also decide and decree a thing, and it will be established for you; and the light [of God's favour] will shine upon your ways.*"

The Pulpit commentary[7] explains that whatever you resolve upon, God will ratify with *His* authority and bring it to pass in due time for your benefit—a promise that carries "a touch of audacity."

Similarly, Matthew Poole's commentary[8] gives us the same assurances: "*Thy purposes and designs shall not be disappointed, but effected and ratified **by God**; which is a great satisfaction. In all thy counsels, and courses, and actions, God shall give thee the light of his direction and governance, and of comfort and success; and thou shalt not be in such a dark, and doubtful, and perplexed condition as now thou art.*"

These are, in effect, the "right conditions" needed for good fruit to be evident and for our God-given purposes to be realised. Our words serve as the seeds, while God's Word functions as the water that nurtures them. To achieve the results God promises, what we have must be backed by His authority. We cannot rely on our own words or personal desires to dictate our purpose; instead, we must declare from God's Word. In doing so, He uses His authority— His Word and His water—to bring our declarations to fruition and secure success.

This is fundamentally the difference between "manifesting" and *"calling those things that be not as though they were"* (Romans 4:17$^{KJV}$).

Manifesting relies solely on our own power, whereas our declarations of the Word, calls into *this* existence, this earthly realm, that which already exists in the realm where God resides.

I know this may sound like a farfetched idea, but we pray it all the time in the model prayer: "Thy will be done, on earth, as it is in heaven..."
In other words, it already exists in heaven, but needs to made manifest on earth, in this earthly realm.

To reiterate, Matthew 18:18$^{(NIV)}$ says *"Whatever you loose on earth is loosed in heaven"*. This scripture refers to the **authority** to make decisions that are binding on the people of God. Many commentaries unpack this to mean that heaven will **confirm** our declarations. I do not believe this to be true. Heaven is the authority so we come in alignment and agreement with heaven, not the other way around. Remember that the Word **comes from** heaven, not from earth.

When we understand that our words on earth, have impact, yet, without the right conditions they are not binding in heaven, even if it is enforced on earth. We need to know that God is not obligated to enforce a word simply because we use His name. He can only use his authority behind a word, when that word matches what's already in heaven.

Ultimately, these arguments show the powerful impact of the right words.

Unless we declare the promises of God that are locked up in His word, they will never take root in our lives, and we cannot expect to experience the fulfilment of His wonderful promises here and now. We must speak these promises consistently and prayerfully, even amid pain, grief, loss, sickness, disappointment, rejection, loneliness, and fear, in order to reap both the spiritual and natural benefits that flow from them.

When we fully grasp the revelation and importance of regularly declaring God's word, it becomes much more than a double-edged sword—it transforms into a force as potent as fire and as powerful as a hammer. As Jeremiah 23:29 *(NIV)* declares, "Is not my word like fire, and like a hammer that breaks a rock in pieces?" The power of God's Word is limitless, capable of providing exactly what we need at any moment.

I am also reminded of Psalm 46:1, which reassures us that God is a very present help in times of need, a promise made real through His word. Furthermore, Jeremiah 1:12*(NIV)* affirms, *"You have observed correctly," says the Lord, "for I am watching over My word to perform it."* Consider this: God is ever-watchful, ready to release His word so that it may be established in our lives. Child of God, what are we waiting for? Wherever you are, even if your situation seems unchangeable, begin to speak and declare that transformation is on its way, countering the enemy's voice with the promise of deliverance.

# I DECREE AND DECLARE

---

I decree and declare that my God is for me and with me, and I shall prevail in Jesus' mighty name! Supernatural safety, protection, and preservation are mine; I am kept secure under the feathers of His wings, and I am protected to fulfil His divine purpose for my life. Every enemy that threatens my physical, emotional, and spiritual well-being is being destroyed at this very moment by the fire of the Holy Spirit. All their schemes designed to cause harm, injury, and destruction are uprooted, dismantled, and rendered null and void. They shall never succeed in carrying out their evil intentions over my life, in Jesus' mighty name.

**Scripture references:** Romans 8:31, Psalm 91:4:, Job 22:28

# 4

# THE POWER OF THE SPOKEN WORD

Declaring God's Authority in Faith

---

Words hold immense power in the spiritual realm, shaping destinies, shifting atmospheres, and unlocking divine authority. The Bible is clear that life and death are in the power of the tongue, and Jesus Himself demonstrated this truth by speaking with authority to situations, nature, and even the enemy.

In this chapter, we explore the biblical foundation of spoken declarations, the divine authority we inherit through Christ, and how aligning our words with God's truth empowers us to walk in victory. When we understand the significance of our speech and the conditions necessary for effective declarations, we can confidently wield the Word of God as a weapon against the forces of darkness and as a key to unlocking His promises in our lives.

Isaiah 55:11[NIV] affirms the unstoppable power of God's word, stating, *"so is my word that goes out from my mouth: It will not return to me empty but will accomplish what I desire and achieve the purpose for which I sent it."* This scripture makes it clear that when the word is declared, it carries the authority to fulfil God's preordained plan.

In a similar vein, Genesis 1:1-3[NIV] documents the creative power of God's spoken word: *"In the beginning God created heaven and the earth... And God said, let there be light: and there was light."* Here, we see how God's word transformed a formless void into a structured, life-sustaining world. Together, these passages powerfully support the idea that the words that proceed from God's mouth are never in vain; they are effective and purposeful, always bringing forth life and achieving the divine intent.

We also see the Son of God demonstrating the immense power and authority of speaking the word. Mark 11:12-14[NIV] tells us clearly about an incident involving Jesus and a fig tree:

*"The next day as they were leaving Bethany, Jesus was hungry. Seeing in the distance a fig tree in leaf, he went to find out if it had any fruit. When he reached it, he found nothing but leaves, because it was not the season for figs. Then he said to the tree, 'May no one ever eat fruit from you again.' And his disciples heard him say it."*

The story continues in verses 20-23[NIV], where we witness the remarkable outcome of Jesus's words:

*"In the morning, as they went along, they saw the fig tree withered from the roots. Peter remembered and said to Jesus, 'Rabbi, look!*

*The fig tree you cursed has withered!' Jesus responded, 'Have faith in God. Truly I tell you, if anyone says to this mountain, "Go, throw yourself into the sea," and does not doubt in their heart but believes that what they say will happen, it will be done for them. "*

It is particularly interesting to notice that before Jesus began to teach His disciples about prayer and faith, He first taught them about the authority and power of spoken words. Through this incident with the fig tree, Jesus provided a vivid example of how words spoken with faith can directly impact and alter reality.

Since we have been adopted into the family of God through faith in Christ Jesus, it naturally follows that we should operate in the same manner as He did, by exercising the authority and power entrusted to us through our spoken words. This is clearly affirmed in John 1:12-13[(((NKJV)))], which states, *"But to all who did receive Him, who believed in His name, He gave the right to become children of God—children born not of blood, nor of the will of the flesh, nor of the will of man, but born of God. "*

As children of God, born of His Spirit and adopted into His divine family, we now share in His authority and nature. Because of this new divine heritage, our words carry profound significance. Just as Jesus demonstrated through His declaration to the fig tree, we too have been given authority through faith in Him. When we speak in alignment with the Word of God, we actively participate in our heavenly inheritance, exercising our God-given right to shape and transform our lives and circumstances.

1 John 4:17[KJV] tells us clearly, *"As He is, so are we in this world. "* Through Christ, we have been given a new identity, one in which

our spiritual DNA has been fundamentally transformed. This new identity reflects the supernatural power, reality, culture, and values of God's kingdom. We no longer belong merely to the realm of the natural but have been made part of an extraordinary, unshakable kingdom. Our very nature and identity have shifted to align with God's supernatural authority, as our spiritual DNA is now patterned after Christ himself.

Scripture reassures us that this divine exchange has taken place: His righteousness has replaced our unrighteousness, and His strength has taken the place of our weakness. We are no longer bound to our former selves but empowered with His heavenly nature. Praise God!

A powerful example of this authority at work can be seen when Jesus Himself was confronted by the devil—the tempter—after He had fasted and prayed for forty days in the wilderness. The Bible records that Jesus was hungry, and in that moment of physical vulnerability, the devil challenged Him, saying, *"If you are the Son of God, command these stones to become bread."* Jesus responded to the devil not with His own reasoning, feelings, or desires, but by directly declaring scripture, saying, *"It is written: Man shall not live by bread alone, but by every word that proceeds from the mouth of God."*

Here, Jesus demonstrates precisely how we, too, can overcome the enemy's temptations and attacks—by boldly and clearly speaking and declaring the Word of God. Jesus overcame through the spoken word, intentionally and decisively applying scripture, thus revealing to us the model of victory over the enemy. This account highlights the importance of speaking and declaring God's word

45

in every challenging situation, affirming our identity and authority in Christ.

Jesus understood clearly that overcoming temptation wasn't merely about resisting the enemy or quoting scripture. He knew all too well, that even words found in scripture could be used carelessly, and aimlessly, and thus have no effect.

Jesus knew that *submission* needed to *precede* resistance, in order for the enemy to flee. He had just come from an intense time of surrender and submission as He underwent His 40 days of fasting. Fasting, by its nature, involves denying the physical needs of the body, which can help to subdue the desires of the flesh and bring the body into submission.

Christ Himself, came into alignment with scripture, as according to James 4:7[(NIV)] *"Submit yourselves, then, to God. Resist the devil, and he will flee from you."*

The Son of God, surrendered His flesh, in submission, and in prayer. Jesus, *"who, being in very nature God, did not consider equality with God something to be used to His own advantage,"* (Philippians 2:6[(NIV)]) submitted Himself to God, in reverence to *His* will and authority.

Jesus knew all too well that *"the spirit indeed is willing, but the flesh is weak", which is why He encourages, and modelled for us to "watch and pray, lest we enter into temptation." (Matt 26:41[KJV])*

46

# 5

# SPEAK THE WORD

The Key to True Prosperity and Success

---

Exodus 7:1[(NIV)] *"Then the LORD said to Moses, "See, I have made you like God to Pharaoh, and your brother Aaron will be your prophet."*

In the book of Exodus, we learn that Moses was "as God" to Pharaoh in that he was the person who revealed God's will. Pharaoh was to be the executor of that will. Aaron would be Moses' prophet as he stood between Moses and Pharaoh and communicated Moses and God's will to the king.

But when Moses dies, and Joshua is poised to take over leading Gods people to the promised land, God says *"Moses My servant is dead. Now therefore, arise, go..."*

God sends Joshua to complete the mission He had started with Moses, but gave him the second half of the instruction He gave to Moses initially:

Deuteronomy 11:1, 8,13,18-21<sup>(((NKJV)))</sup>

*"Love the Lord your God and keep his requirements, his decrees, his laws and his commands always...Observe therefore all the commands I am giving you today... faithfully obey the commands I am giving you today ... Fix these words of mine in your hearts and minds; tie them as symbols on your hands and bind them on your foreheads. Teach them to your children, talking about them when you sit at home and when you walk along the road, when you lie down and when you get up. Write them on the doorframes of your houses and on your gates, so that your days and the days of your children may be many in the land the Lord swore to give your ancestors, as many as the days that the heavens are above the earth."*

The first half of the instruction was to familiarise themselves with the Word, to know it intimately, to have it ingrained in them, to teach it to their children. They needed to see it wherever they were and wherever they went. They needed to know what the word was, in order to fully obey it.

The result of familiarising themselves with the word and obeying the instruction, was God's promise of provision: *"then I will send rain on your land in its season, both autumn and spring rains, so that you may gather in your grain, new wine and olive oil. I will provide grass in the fields for your cattle, and you will eat and be satisfied"*- Deuteronomy 11:14[(NIV)]

However, when God instructed Joshua on how to become prosperous and successful, He emphasised a profound principle. God did not simply tell Joshua to read or quietly reflect on the scriptures— this was already established under the rule of Moses— He commanded Joshua to take it a step further and to *speak the Word continually.*

Joshua 1:8[KJV] clearly says, *"This book of the law shall not depart out of thy mouth; but thou shalt meditate therein day and night, that thou mayest observe to do according to all that is written therein: for then thou shalt make thy way prosperous, and then thou shalt have good success."*

When we put these instructions together and look at the bigger picture, it reveals the "right conditions" or the essential keys: true success and prosperity are directly connected to speaking God's Word aloud and meditating upon it consistently. This however, needs to be preceded by studying and understanding the Word, and having a genuine love for the God of the Word. Once we have those foundational things established, and we deliberately speak and continually reflect on scripture, it not only transforms our thoughts but empowers us to act according to God's guidance. Speaking the Word strengthens our spirit, helps us resist temptation, and builds our confidence in God's promises.

Meditating on God's Word means more than merely reading it silently; it involves regularly declaring it aloud until it becomes part of us. This is how faith is built. Romans 10:17[(NKJV)]says, *"So*

49

*then faith comes by hearing, and hearing by the word of God.*"
The purpose of declaring a thing audibly, is not to "throw it out
to the u(NIV)erse", but it is so that we can *hear* it, as we speak it.
This intentional practice ensures that our hearts, minds, and
circumstances align with His divine purposes. By making a habit
of verbally declaring scripture day and night, we immerse
ourselves in God's truth, enabling it to take root deeply within us;
and the more we hear it, the more and deeper we believe it. The
result is a life of boldness and strength in God, which positions us
to experience His favour and blessing, granting us genuine
prosperity and lasting success.

## Speaking Life into Hopeless Situations

In Ezekiel 37:3-10[(((NKJV)))], we encounter a remarkable story
demonstrating the power of spoken words aligned with God's
instruction.

*"And He said to me, "Son of man, can these bones live?"*

*So I answered, "O Lord God, You know.*

*Again He said to me, "Prophesy to these bones, and say to them,
'O dry bones, hear the word of the Lord! Thus says the
Lord God to these bones: "Surely I will cause breath to enter into
you, and you shall live. I will put sinews on you and bring flesh
upon you, cover you with skin and put breath in you; and you
shall live. Then you shall know that I am the Lord."'"*

*So I prophesied as I was commanded; and as I prophesied, there
was a noise, and suddenly a rattling; and the bones came together,*

*bone to bone. Indeed, as I looked, the sinews and the flesh came upon them, and the skin covered them over; but there was no breath in them.*

*Also He said to me, "Prophesy to the breath, prophesy, son of man, and say to the breath, 'Thus says the Lord God: "Come from the four winds, O breath, and breathe on these slain, that they may live."'' "So, I prophesied as He commanded me, and breath came into them, and they lived, and stood upon their feet, an exceedingly great army."*

As Ezekiel obeyed and spoke these prophetic declarations, what had once been utterly hopeless, barren, and lifeless became a mighty, living army.

Ezekiel chose to partner *with* God by speaking as he had been instructed.

This leads us to yet another condition that needs to be met: Partnership with God.

The Bible further emphasises the significance of verbal declarations in Psalm 107, verse 2[KJV,] stating, "*Let the redeemed of the Lord say so, whom he hath redeemed from the hand of the enemy.*" Is this not a powerful reminder to us? When we reflect upon all the goodness, mercy, and favour that God has shown us, how can we remain silent and not declare His faithfulness aloud?

Therefore, before you continue, I encourage you to affirm these truths out loud: "I am loved, I am special, I am enough, and I am worth dying for. I am so valuable that Christ willingly gave His life for me. I am worthy, accepted, and cherished by God."

As we journey further into this teaching, we will grow increasingly mindful of the power within our words and declarations, becoming more aware of the tangible, supernatural presence of Yahweh Nissi in our daily lives.

Hebrew 1:3[NIV]
*"The Son is the radiance of God's glory and the exact representation of his being, sustaining all things by his powerful word."*

# 6

# SUPERNATURAL SAFETY AND DIVINE PROTECTION

## A Covenant of Security in Christ

---

The extent and intensity of mankind's sin and the resulting curse have profoundly impacted the perfect creation of God, introducing corruption and chaos. This corruption has transformed our world into a place filled with danger, where people face daily suffering from natural disasters, crime, accidents, poor health, and countless other adversities. The effects of humanity's fallen state are felt in every corner of the earth, causing pain, uncertainty, and fear.

Consequently, the need for safety and protection has become a fundamental part of everyday human life. Everyone seeks security from threats and harm, longing to live free from constant danger and worry. Divine protection, therefore, becomes not only appealing but essential for navigating through life.

## What is Supernatural Safety and Protection?

David Ibiyeomie[9] (2013,8), in his book *Understanding Divine Protection*, defines divine protection as *"the act of supernaturally shielding someone from harm, injury or danger. It is God's way of defending or shielding man from every form of evil; it is supreme and absolutely dependable."*

This explanation beautifully captures the very essence of divine protection—God actively and supernaturally intervening to shield and preserve humanity from danger, harm, and the threat of destruction.

In the world and era we are living in today, God's divine protection is not merely desirable but absolutely essential. It is His personal assurance of our safety amidst the chaos and uncertainty of life.

As we journey through the pages of this book, we will closely examine God's promises concerning divine safety and protection. By doing so, we will become more aware of the covenantal rights we hold as children of God. Scripture explicitly reminds us in John 15:19 that we are *"not of the world,"* but rather chosen and set apart by Christ Himself. Divine protection is your rightful inheritance through Christ, who shed His blood to ensure your safety and preservation. Understanding this truth enables us to confidently exercise our rights as heirs of the Kingdom, particularly when it comes to supernatural protection and safety. You can confidently claim this protection and boldly declare God's word in the face of adversity. The prophetic power locked within these declarations will break the power of darkness and establish God's supernatural authority in your life.

As we declare and speak out God's promises regarding divine protection, we engage the powerful authority invested in our tongues—the power that brings life or death into every circumstance. By speaking *deliberately* and *intentionally* against every wicked assignment designed to harm, injure, or destroy us, we nullify their evil mandates and dismantle their strategies. Our words, inspired by faith and backed by scriptural authority, can uproot, disrupt, and completely destroy the plans of darkness. This truth, when fully embraced, gives us the boldness to speak out with authority, using our words intentionally and prophetically.

The enemy is constantly searching for opportunities to threaten, harm, and instil fear in our hearts. His primary objective is to steal our peace, kill our joy, and destroy our sense of security. As we experience daily reports of crime, murder, rape, and gang violence, it's natural for us to feel apprehensive, thinking subconsciously that perhaps we, or our friends and family members, might become victims of these horrendous acts. It was this reality that deeply moved me to address this critical issue in this book—to remind us of the greater and more powerful reality of God's Kingdom, which dwells within us, giving us the authority to reject fear and hopelessness.

We must remain continually aware that the enemy seeks opportunities to intimidate and paralyse us with fear, attempting to overshadow the divine truth residing in our spirits. However, through deliberate and consistent daily declarations of God's

Word, we release powerful, inspired prophetic confessions that shape and transform our circumstances. Indeed, the Word of God is alive and active, hallelujah! It penetrates deeply, dismantling every dark intention of the enemy and establishing divine peace and security in our hearts and lives.

There is tremendous power at work when we consistently declare and affirm God's promises over ourselves, our communities, and loved ones.

As Psalm 4:8$^{NLT}$ confidently proclaims, *"In peace I will lie down and sleep, for you alone, O LORD, will keep me safe."* This promise reassures us that divine protection is real, accessible, and dependable. Furthermore, Isaiah 54:17$^{(NIV)}$ solidifies our understanding of this supernatural protection, promising us that, *"No weapon forged against you will prevail, and you will refute every tongue that accuses you. This is the heritage of the servants of the Lord, and this is their vindication from me,"* declares the Lord."

It's also important to recognise that God's protective covering extends beyond mere physical safety; it encompasses our spiritual, emotional, and mental well-being as well.

Let's now explore further, through scriptural examples, how God's supernatural protection secures and guards us completely—spiritually, emotionally, mentally, and physically—in every aspect of our lives.

## God's Comprehensive Protection of Our Soul

Proverbs 4:23[NIV] urges us, "*Above all else, guard your heart, for everything you do flows from it.*" This highlights how critical our spiritual and emotional protection is.

Psalm 121:7-8[NIV] confirms this further, declaring, "*The Lord will keep you from all harm—he will watch over your life; the Lord will watch over your coming and going both now and forevermore.*" Interestingly, the Hebrew word used in this verse, "נַפְשֶׁךָ" (nafshecha) specifically refers to the soul, indicating that God's protection extends to our innermost being, (Chabad, 2025)[10]. This suggests that God's protective care reaches deeply into our very inner selves, shielding our hearts and minds from harm and internal distress, ensuring our innermost being is safe and secure under His vigilant care.

## Emotional and Mental Protection:

In Isaiah 41:10[NIV], God further emphasises His complete protection by saying, "*So do not fear, for I am with you; do not be dismayed, for I am your God. I will strengthen you and help you; I will uphold you with my righteous right hand.*" This powerful reassurance directly addresses emotional and mental protection, promising God's continuous strength and steadfast presence to combat fear, anxiety, and despair.

Likewise, Philippians 4:6-7[NIV] addresses emotional protection with great clarity: "*Do not be anxious about anything, but in everything by prayer and supplication with thanksgiving let your requests be made known to God. And the peace of God, which*

57

*surpasses all understanding, will guard your hearts and your minds in Christ Jesus.*" Here the scripture beautifully illustrates that the peace of God serves as a shield, actively guarding our hearts and minds against anxiety, stress, and fear, preserving us emotionally and spiritually.

Thus, these verses clearly demonstrate God's loving intention to provide us with complete protection—encompassing our souls, minds, emotions, and spirits—ensuring that we live confidently and peacefully, assured of His supernatural safety and preservation.

## Spiritual Protection:

**Spiritual protection** is clearly illustrated in Ephesians 6:11-17, where the Apostle Paul speaks of putting on the whole armour of God, which equips us spiritually for daily battles against unseen forces. This armour includes the belt of truth, the breastplate of righteousness, feet fitted with readiness from the gospel of peace, the shield of faith, the helmet of salvation, and the sword of the Spirit, which is the Word of God. Through this spiritual armour, God provides us with divine protection from the enemy's attempts to attack, influence, or harm us spiritually.

Psalm 91:1-2[NIV] beautifully echoes this theme of supernatural protection, affirming that: "*Whoever dwells in the shelter of the Most High will rest in the shadow of the Almighty. I will say of the Lord, 'He is my refuge and my fortress, my God, in whom I trust.'*" The Psalmist declares confidently that those who remain intimately connected to God will experience His constant and secure protection. This speaks of God not merely as a distant protector, but as a close, personal refuge, sheltering us from spiritual harm and comforting us during turbulent times. It highlights the personal aspect of God's commitment to protect us, emphasising our complete safety within His presence.

## Protection from Spiritual Harm:

Protection from spiritual harm is powerfully demonstrated in Romans 8:38-39[NIV], where the Apostle Paul declares, "*For I am convinced that neither death nor life, neither angels nor demons, neither the present nor the future, nor any powers, neither height nor depth, nor anything else in all creation, will be able to separate us from the love of God that is in Christ Jesus our Lord.*" This passage beautifully emphasises the absolute assurance of our spiritual security, confirming that nothing—no spiritual force, circumstance, or created thing—can ever remove us from the protective embrace of God's unfailing love.

These scriptures collectively illustrate the comprehensive nature of God's divine protection, affirming His care for our physical, spiritual, emotional, and mental well-being.

It is also worth noting that God's unfailing and unconditional love sometimes extends beyond His people, causing even those who do not know Him to experience His goodness, safety, protection, and preservation due to His sovereign grace. Matthew 5:45[NKJV] captures this truth, stating, "*He causes his sun to rise on the evil and the good and sends rain on the righteous and the unrighteous,*" demonstrating God's generosity and mercy toward all humanity.

Yet, it remains true that the full measure of God's absolute divine protection and preservation can only be experienced in and through Jesus Christ. He alone is the certain path to experiencing the complete security and safety promised to us by our Heavenly Father.

**7**

# THE PROMISES OF DIVINE PROTECTION

## God's Unwavering Shield Over His People

---

The Bible is filled with numerous scriptures that beautifully reveal God's promises regarding His divine protection and safety for His people. Let us explore a few powerful examples from Scripture that clearly validate these promises.

Psalm 121:7-8 says, *"The LORD will protect you from all evil; God will protect your very life. The LORD will protect you on your journeys— whether going or coming— from now until forever."* Revised Standard Version (NRSV)

The Hebrew root for the verb "protect" in this verse is **shamar**, which carries deep meaning. It first appears in Genesis 2:15, where Adam is instructed to tend and "guard" the Garden of Eden. It also appears in Genesis 17:9, where God commands Abraham to "keep" His covenant. According to John J. Parsons[11] (2023) from *Hebrew 4 Christians*, the word **shamar** is used more than 400 times throughout the Tanakh, highlighting its significant meaning as "exercising great care over," "watching over," "guarding," "taking heed," and even "tending carefully" like a shepherd watching over his flock.

This rich Hebrew word assures us profoundly of God's careful attention and deliberate care toward us. Like a mother hen carefully watches over her chicks, God proactively guards and watches over us. He is never anxious or caught off guard, for He is omnipresent (always present) and omniscient (all-knowing). He is actively monitoring every potential threat from the kingdom of darkness that seeks to cause harm, injury, premature death, and destruction.

In addition, Psalm 34:7[(ESV)] further emphasises the active and supernatural protection of God: *"The angel of the LORD encamps around those who fear him and delivers them."* This verse vividly illustrates God's protection, with heavenly hosts surrounding us to ensure our deliverance from danger. These scriptures powerfully affirm and reinforce God's unwavering promise to shield and guard us at every moment.

### The following scriptures further affirm and highlight God's divine commitment to protecting His people:

In Daniel 6:22[(ESV)], we see Daniel testifying to God's supernatural protection: *"My God sent his angel and shut the lions' mouths, and they have not harmed me because I was found blameless*

*before him; and also before you, O king, I have done no harm."*
Here we clearly observe God's supernatural intervention, protecting Daniel from certain death because of his righteousness and unwavering trust in God.

In Job 1:10[((NKJV))], the Bible gives us another example of how God safeguards His faithful: *"Have you not put a hedge around him and his house and all that he has, on every side? You have blessed the work of his hands, and his possessions have increased in the land."* This scripture depicts a protective barrier established by God Himself, safeguarding His servant from harm and facilitating prosperity and increase.

Furthermore, Psalm 34:7[(NKJV)] assures us, *"The angel of the LORD encamps around those who fear him, and delivers them,"* highlighting once again the divine protection that surrounds and preserves God's people.

God's assurance of protection is also beautifully expressed in Isaiah 41:10[((NKJV))], *"Fear not, for I am with you; be not dismayed, for I am your God; I will strengthen you, I will help you, I will uphold you with my righteous right hand."* This verse reaffirms that divine protection is accompanied by strength, support, and comfort in times of trouble.

Romans 8:31-32[(NIV)] encourages us, declaring, "If God is for us, who can be against us? He who did not spare his own Son but gave him up for us all, how will he not also with him graciously give us all things?" This scripture reminds us of the immeasurable extent of God's protective love, demonstrating that if God sacrificed His Son for us, He would undoubtedly provide protection and safety.

Moreover, Isaiah 41:10$^{(NIV)}$ comforts us with this reassuring promise: *"Fear not, for I am with you; be not dismayed, for I am your God; I will strengthen you, I will help you, I will uphold you with my righteous right hand."* The promise contained here reminds us of God's personal and intentional commitment to shield and protect us from harm.

Likewise, John 3:16$^{(NIV)}$ reiterates the greatest act of divine protection, stating, *"For God so loved the world, that he gave his only Son, that whoever believes in him should not perish but have eternal life."* God's ultimate protective act was giving Christ to secure our eternal safety, offering us the guarantee of everlasting life.

Psalm 146:3-5$^{(NIV)}$ warns against placing our ultimate trust in people or earthly powers, encouraging us instead to rely upon God alone, who is eternally trustworthy and able to provide real and lasting protection: *"Put not your trust in princes, in a son of man, in whom there is no salvation... Blessed is he whose help is the God of Jacob, whose hope is in the LORD his God."*

Finally, Matthew 11:28$^{(NKJV)}$comforts us in our anxieties, offering rest and divine peace: *"Come to me, all who labour and are heavy laden, and I will give you rest."* Moreover, 1 Peter 5:7$^{(NIV)}$ urges us to cast our anxieties upon God, promising that He genuinely cares for us and desires our wellbeing: *"Cast all your anxiety on him because he cares for you."*

Together, these scriptures form an undeniable foundation of confidence, reminding us continually that supernatural safety, divine protection, and preservation remain accessible realities for all who belong to Christ Jesus.

## Declaration and Affirmation of Supernatural Safety and Divine Protection using the above scriptures:

I declare boldly, in the powerful and matchless name of Jesus Christ, that God has commanded His angels to guard and protect me, as He did for Daniel in the lions' den (Daniel 6:22). The Lord has set a divine hedge around my family, my home, and all that concerns me; His blessing is evident in everything I set my hands to do, causing me to flourish and prosper in every area of my life (Job 1:10).

In every moment of trouble or uncertainty, the Lord Himself will conceal me in the safety of His shelter, hide me securely under the cover of His tent, and position me upon a high rock, out of the reach of harm (Psalm 27:5). I confidently declare that I am deeply loved by God, who sent His only Son, Jesus Christ, to die for me, giving me the guarantee of eternal life and everlasting safety in Him (John 3:16).

Today, I reject all fear, anxiety, and discouragement, declaring that my God is with me, strengthening and helping me, upholding me with His righteous right hand (Isaiah 41:10). I choose to be strong and courageous, refusing to dread or fear any enemy or situation because my Lord goes before me, promising never to leave or forsake me (Deuteronomy 31:6).

I consciously cast all my anxieties and cares upon God, knowing that He deeply and genuinely cares for me (1 Peter 5:7). I am convinced, beyond any doubt, that since God is for me, absolutely nothing and no one can successfully stand against me. The same God who freely gave up His own Son for my sake will graciously and generously supply all my needs and protect me from harm (Romans 8:31-32).

With unwavering faith, I declare that my Father can instantly release legions of angels at my disposal, ensuring supernatural deliverance, protection, and victory in any circumstance (Matthew 26:53).

Therefore, I praise the Lord continually with my whole being, placing my trust completely in Him alone, and confidently relying on His protection, because my help, hope, and safety are securely found in the God of Jacob, the Lord my God (Psalm 146:1-149:9).

**He is the Lord our banner.**

In Exodus 17:15[(NIV)], scripture records: "*Moses built an altar and called it The LORD is my Banner.*" The name **Yahweh Nissi** is the name that symbolises God's protective presence and divine guidance over His people. Moses chose this powerful name following a miraculous victory that God granted to Israel over the Amalekites.

As we stated earlier, in ancient warfare, armies commonly raised a banner or flag attached to a pole, giving their soldiers a clear focal point—a sign to unite and rally around during intense battles. Similarly, when we place our focus upon God, making Him the central point of our attention during times of distress, fear, discouragement, or when facing any threat—whether natural or spiritual—we position ourselves to experience the full measure of His deliverance, protection, and victory. Yahweh Nissi assures us that when He is our banner, we are never alone or without help, but instead, we stand confidently under His powerful defence.

## Declaration of Supernatural Safety and Divine Protection:

I boldly declare according to **Isaiah 54:17,** that no weapon formed against me shall prosper, and every accusing tongue will be silenced. This promise is my rightful inheritance and vindication from the Lord.

According to **Isaiah 41:11-12,** I affirm that all who rage against me will be utterly ashamed and disgraced. Those who oppose me will become powerless and be brought to nothing; they will vanish, and I will look for them but not find them, because God Himself fights on my behalf.

I confidently affirm **Psalm 121:7-8,** declaring that the Lord watches over every aspect of my life, protecting me from all harm and danger. Whether I am coming or going, His vigilant and constant presence preserves me today and forevermore.

According to **2 Thessalonians 3:3,** I declare that my Lord is faithful; He continually strengthens and shields me from every scheme of the evil one. My safety is secure, and I stand firm in His divine protection.

Standing on **2 Timothy 4:18,** I affirm with absolute trust that the Lord will rescue me from every evil attack and bring me safely into His heavenly kingdom. Nothing designed against me can disrupt God's plan of protection and deliverance for my life.

Finally, I declare **Psalm 91** over my life: I dwell securely in the shelter of the Most High and rest safely in the shadow of the Almighty. The Lord Himself is my refuge and fortress, the God in whom I fully trust. He rescues me from hidden dangers and protects me from deadly diseases. He covers me lovingly with His feathers, shielding me under His wings, and His faithfulness surrounds me like a strong shield. Therefore, I will not fear terror at night or threats by day; no plague, pestilence, or destruction will overtake me. His angels surround me, lifting me above danger, enabling me to overcome every spiritual enemy. Because God is my protector, He promises to answer my prayers, deliver me from harm, honour me, grant me long life, and reveal to me the fullness of His salvation.

## God Our Refuge and Fortress

According to Ralph F. Wilson[12], God is described in Scripture as our Rock, our Shade, and our Hiding Place. This metaphor was especially meaningful in ancient times, where people frequently faced dangers from bandits and raiding gangs who would attack vulnerable villages—taking their possessions, harming the inhabitants, and even enslaving or killing them.

In response to such threats, Scripture uses powerful imagery to convey how God offers protection. For instance, God is called a "Rock," represented by the Hebrew word *tsûr,* which refers to massive boulders or solid rock formations that form mountains. These rocky caves were the actual shelters where David and his men hid safely while being pursued by King Saul's forces. God is also referred to by another Hebrew word, sela, meaning "split rock" or "cleft rock." This term highlights places of shelter, such as crevices or cliffs, providing refuge from harm.

Both these Hebrew terms for "rock" vividly portray God Himself as our secure and impenetrable place of refuge, where we can safely hide when facing danger. This imagery is further expanded in the New Testament, where Christ is explicitly referred to as our Rock (see 1 Peter 2:6; 1 Corinthians 10:4), underscoring His role as our firm foundation and safe refuge.

Additionally, the Hebrew word seter, meaning "hiding place," is another significant term describing the personal and intimate shelter God provides to His people. It reflects the comfort and absolute safety found uniquely in the presence and protection of God.

Furthermore, Wilson explains that the Hebrew word metsûdâ, meaning "fortress" or "stronghold," is closely related to the word metsād, signifying a "mountain height" or "summit." The famous fortress-palace of Masada, built by Herod the Great near the Dead Sea, derives its name from this word. In the scriptures (1 Samuel 23:14, 19, and 29), David frequently sought refuge from King Saul by hiding within these mountainous fortresses or strongholds. This imagery vividly demonstrates how God Himself serves as our mighty fortress, protecting us securely and effectively from every threat or attack. Similarly, God is described as our Rock, our Shade, and our Hiding Place, further emphasising His role as our divine protector. In ancient times, villages were constantly at risk from violent raiders and bandits who would attack, plunder, and destroy unprotected settlements. In these dangerous circumstances, God was understood as a secure and immovable rock (tsûr), representing massive formations or mountain boulders in which one could safely hide. David's experience, hiding in rocky caves from Saul, reinforces this powerful metaphor. Additionally, God is referred to as sela, meaning a "split rock" or "cleft in the rock," symbolising a personal and secure refuge where individuals find protection. The New Testament continues this theme, explicitly identifying Christ as our Rock.

Moreover, Scripture describes God as our Shield and Buckler, highlighting His role as our defensive armour. The Hebrew word *māgēn*[13] refers to a smaller round shield used by infantry and officers, emphasising a shield that actively protects from imminent danger.

Another term, *sinnâ*, describes a large rectangular shield providing full-body coverage. The word *sōchērā*, translated as "buckler," signifies a smaller, more agile shield designed for close combat, related to the Hebrew root *sāchar*, meaning "to surround or encircle." Lastly, the Hebrew word *chereb* refers to a sword or dagger, underscoring the proactive nature of God's protection— both defensive and offensive—against threats.

These powerful scriptural metaphors collectively demonstrate that God alone is our comprehensive and reliable protector, capable of shielding us from every form of harm, injury, or danger. These images reveal the depth of His loving care and His unwavering commitment to keep us safe and secure in all circumstances.

Wilson, writing at Jesuswalk.com[12], further states that in Old Testament times—particularly before the Roman period brought relative peace to Palestine—the need for a refuge or fortress was genuinely critical and urgent. Unprotected villages were often built around fortified cities, allowing residents to quickly retreat and find safety during unexpected attacks or warfare. These strongholds were strategically built with high towers, sturdy walls, and secure gates, creating safe havens that shielded villagers from attackers.

Two Hebrew terms stand out in scripture, vividly illustrating God as our refuge and fortress. The first, *machseh*, derives from the Hebrew root *chāsā*, meaning "to seek refuge" or "flee for protection." This vividly captures the action of turning toward God in times of imminent danger. Another important term is *metsûdâ*, closely related to *metsād,* meaning "mountain height" or "summit." Historically, fortresses such as Masada—built by Herod near the Dead Sea—were located strategically on mountain summits, ensuring their security and making them nearly impossible for enemies to breach. Scripture references such fortresses repeatedly, as David sought refuge in mountain strongholds (metsād) when pursued by King Saul.

Together, these metaphors clearly depict God's unwavering, steadfast protection, highlighting His role as our impenetrable refuge. He stands as our strong fortress, providing security from harm, danger, and every form of attack. These scriptural examples vividly confirm that God alone is our true source of protection. He is indeed our ultimate shield and impenetrable fortress, guarding us against harm in both the spiritual and natural realms. Isaiah 60:2[(NKJV)]emphasises this promise: *"For behold, darkness shall cover the earth, and gross darkness the people; but the LORD shall arise upon you, and his glory shall be seen upon you."*

While darkness—manifesting as fear, crime, violence, and despair—may indeed envelop the world, God's promise remains steadfast, assuring us that His radiant presence and divine protection will be clearly evident upon His people. God's divine glory, defined as His manifested presence, honour, splendour, and majesty, serves as our supernatural covering, guarding us from harm. Even in these turbulent and uncertain times, God Himself remains our permanent refuge, always available and eager to shield and guard us against every threat and danger.

Now, more than ever, it is vital for us to wholeheartedly embrace and walk confidently in the reality of God's supernatural presence and protective care. When we allow His glory—His weighty, honourable, splendid, and tangible manifested presence—to envelop our lives, we become fully shielded, sustained, and transformed.

# 8

# PROTECTED AND PRESERVED

The Purpose Behind God's Divine Shield

While writing, I began to notice and understand that the words **protection** and **preservation** sometimes share the same meaning. I've also observed that in some scriptures, as well as across various translations, these words are often used interchangeably, conveying essentially the same idea. At times, the meaning clearly emphasises protection—keeping someone away from harm—and at other times, preservation highlights the idea of keeping someone alive. Therefore, for the purpose of this book, we will embrace both meanings, understanding these terms as implying God's active role in keeping us alive and safe from harm.

When we experience God's divine hand of protection and preservation, it's usually linked directly to a divine purpose, while simultaneously ensuring our safety as His beloved children. Just like any loving parent, God is deeply concerned about our safety and wellbeing.

Here are some reasons why God protects and preserves us:

## His unconditional love

John 3:16[NKJV]illustrates this so clearly to all of us: *"For God so loved the world, that he gave his only Son, that whoever believes in him should not perish but have eternal life."* This love has never depended, nor will it ever depend, upon anything we can do to earn or deserve it. It is a love so profound and so deep that it was visibly demonstrated to all humanity through God's giving of His one and only Son for our redemption and justification.

God's love is beautifully described by the Greek word **agapao**[14], which means unconditional and preferential love—a love deliberately chosen and acted out by God's will. Because of this supernatural and unconditional love, divine protection and preservation naturally flow toward us.

What a loving and caring heavenly Father we have! If you are reading this book and have never given your life to Jesus Christ, please understand this deeply important truth: He loves you unconditionally, exactly where you are right now. You might feel undeserving of such a powerful, unconditional love because of past mistakes, failures, or sins you've committed. Yet, let me assure you of this truth: you are immensely precious and valuable to Him. So precious, in fact, that He willingly gave His own dear Son as a ransom, exchanging His Son's life for your redemption, justification, and restoration, ensuring that you can have abundant and everlasting life.

## Against evil people and evil forces

All of us would like to believe the best in others, yet we cannot deny the existence of evil people who actively partner with dark spiritual forces to bring about destruction. No matter how uncomfortable this reality is, the truth remains that some individuals harbour wicked intentions and actively seek to bring harm, pain, and suffering into the lives of others. Knowing this, God—who is infinitely wise, compassionate, and sovereign—has provided us with supernatural protection to shield us from such people and their harmful actions.

Esther 3:5-6[(NIV)] illustrates an example of an evil heart in action: *"When Haman saw for himself that Mordecai did not bow down or pay him honour, he was enraged. Yet having learned who Mordecai's people were, he scorned the idea of killing only Mordecai. Instead, Haman looked for a way to destroy all Mordecai's people, the Jews, throughout the whole kingdom of Xerxes."*

This scripture powerfully highlights that some people actively align themselves with evil intentions, mirroring the malicious character of Satan himself. Yet even amid such dark plots, God—in His sovereignty—provides supernatural protection. Sometimes He intervenes miraculously, shielding us from harm, even without our knowledge or awareness.

David expresses this very reality clearly and honestly in Psalm 140:4[(NIV)], crying out to God: *"Keep me, O LORD, from the hands of the wicked; protect me from men of violence who plan to trip my feet."* David's plea highlights the seriousness and reality of the danger posed by evil people and their schemes, reinforcing our dependence upon God's supernatural defence.

Sadly, the influence of evil extends even further, as some people intentionally engage in witchcraft to cause immense suffering, destruction, and loss. Such evil practices might manifest in diverse forms, including premature death, accidents, marital strife, miscarriages, infertility, sickness, job loss, division, or stagnation within families and communities. However, we have a strong assurance from Scripture in Micah 5:12[(NIV)], where God declares His intention clearly: *"I will destroy your witchcraft and you will no longer cast spells."*

Therefore, I boldly declare, in alignment with Micah 5:12, that every evil assignment directed toward your life—aimed at hindering your destiny, destroying your peace, sabotaging your progress, or inflicting harm—is destroyed right now in Jesus' name. Every demonic foundation working against you through witchcraft is dismantled by God's supernatural power. You are shielded, protected, and delivered because divine protection and safety are your covenant rights as a child of God.

Do not fear threats of witchcraft or any evil assignment when you find yourself abiding securely in Christ, the King of glory. May every evil foundation, every wicked plot, and every negative spiritual arrangement against your life be broken and destroyed completely in the mighty name of Jesus Christ.

## The Devil and Evil Forces

Every single human being has been created in the image and likeness of God, and this very fact deeply frustrates and angers Satan because it constantly reminds him of what he lost when he rebelled against God. Scripture clearly records the prideful ambition that led to his downfall in Isaiah 14:12-15[NIV]:

> *"How you are fallen from heaven, O Lucifer, son of the morning! How you are cut down to the ground, you who weakened the nations! For you have said in your heart, 'I will ascend into heaven, I will exalt my throne above the stars of God; I will also sit on the mount of the congregation, on the farthest sides of the north; I will ascend above the heights of the clouds, I will be like the Most High.' Yet you shall be brought down to Sheol, to the lowest depths of the Pit."*

Having lost his place in heaven due to his deliberate rebellion, Satan has since been consumed by hatred, envy, and a relentless desire to harm humanity. As John 10:10[NKJV] warns us, his singular mission is clear:

> *"The thief comes only to steal and kill and destroy; I have come that they may have life, and have it to the full."*

Jesus explicitly cautioned Simon Peter in Luke 22:31[NIV], stating: *"Simon, Simon, Satan has asked to sift all of you as wheat."* This clearly indicates the enemy's relentless desire to harm and disrupt our lives.

77

The Apostle Peter further warns us of the devil's constant and dangerous presence in 1 Peter 5:8[NIV]: *"Be alert and of sober mind. Your enemy the devil prowls around like a roaring lion looking for someone to devour."* This vivid description emphasises the devil's ongoing search for vulnerable individuals to attack and destroy.

Ephesians 6:10-12[NIV] clearly describes our spiritual struggle against these dark forces:

*"Finally, be strong in the Lord and in his mighty power. Put on the full armour of God, so that you can take your stand against the devil's schemes. For our struggle is not against flesh and blood, but against the rulers, against the authorities, against the powers of this dark world, and against the spiritual forces of evil in the heavenly realms."*

Thus, it is clear from these scriptures that the devil, together with his demonic cohorts, has made it his mission to inflict harm, injury, death, sickness, and destruction upon humanity. This aligns precisely with Jesus' words in John 10:10, which state that Satan's ultimate agenda is "to steal, kill, and destroy."

## Protected and Preserved for a Purpose

Genesis 45:5[NKJV] clearly illustrates the reality of God's divine preservation when Joseph declares, *"And now, do not be distressed and do not be angry with yourselves for selling me here, because it was to save lives that God sent me ahead of you."* Joseph was intentionally preserved by God's sovereign authority and power for a greater purpose—to save the lives of many people.

Even though he experienced painful rejection, betrayal, and hardship because of his brothers, God had a higher purpose and plan in place. Joseph's rejection, therefore, was actually orchestrated by God for a significant purpose, highlighting that sometimes disappointments, betrayals, and rejection may indeed be for our own protection and ultimate benefit.

Joseph's life is a vivid example that when we face adversity, we should remain steadfast in our faith, fully assured that God's purpose for our lives cannot be thwarted. Just as Joseph was kept alive and protected to fulfil a greater plan of saving many lives, we also are shielded by God's powerful hand of protection because He has uniquely created each of us for a specific purpose. God's sovereign plan for our lives will come to fruition, despite the difficult circumstances we sometimes endure. As John 16:33[NKJV] clearly states, "*I have told you these things, so that in me you may have peace. In this world you will have trouble. But take heart! I have overcome the world.*" This scripture provides assurance and comfort to believers, reinforcing that even in moments of difficulty, God's greater purpose remains intact.

It is critical to understand that God's divine protection often accompanies the divine purpose He has for each believer's life. The life of Joseph is a testimony of how divine preservation works in tandem with God's divine purpose. Joseph's gifts and purpose preserved not only his own life but also that of his entire family and the lives of many others in the surrounding nations.

This is a reminder that believers will indeed experience trials and challenges, yet should remain confident and faithful, trusting that the Almighty has a distinct plan and purpose for each life.

The Scriptures further emphasise our calling into divine purpose in John 16:33 and Ephesians 2:10, where we are reminded that we are created by God unto good works and destined by Him to fulfil our divine assignments. God's preservation in our lives ensures we remain alive, safe, and protected to complete the good works He has preordained. This is why His mighty hand of protection continues to operate in our lives, preserving us daily and ensuring that we fulfil our God-given destinies.

# TRANSITIONING INTO THE BATTLE

Having explored the authority of your voice and the power of declaring God's Word, we now step into a deeper dimension. Speaking the Word is vital—but understanding the opposition is just as critical. Part 2 will reveal the spiritual forces that resist God's protection and the strategies heaven gives to overcome them. Get ready to discern the enemy's tactics, recognise your spiritual structure, and embrace the full provision of God's protection. This is where warfare meets wisdom, and declarations meet discernment.

# PART 2

# UNDERSTANDING THE BATTLE

This section uncovers the realities of spiritual warfare. God's promise of protection stands firm—but it is often challenged. You'll learn to identify the schemes of the enemy, navigate emotional and spiritual wounds, and see how deliverance plays a vital role in securing your wholeness. These chapters reveal how fear, trauma, and deception open doors to danger, and how faith, authority, and God's design for humanity bring breakthrough. Prepare to move from vulnerability to victory.

# 9

# ANGELIC PROTECTION

## God's Messengers and Guardians

According to the Bible, angels are spiritual beings created by God specifically to serve His purposes. The English word "angel" originates from the Greek word ἄγγελος[15] (*Angelos*), which means "messenger."

Angels carry out various roles throughout Scripture, including delivering important messages to God's people, as seen in Genesis 22:11-22; praising and worshipping God, as described in Isaiah 6:2-3; providing protection for those who belong to God, as highlighted in Psalm 91:11-12; and executing divine judgment, as demonstrated in 2 Kings 19:35.

In the New Testament, angels are frequently seen accompanying Jesus during significant events in His life. They are present at His birth (Luke 1:26-38), minister to Him during His temptation in the wilderness (Matthew 4:11), announce His resurrection from the dead (John 20:11-13), and they will accompany Him again during the final judgment (Matthew 16:27).

Among angels mentioned by name, two are particularly notable in the Bible: Gabriel, who stands directly in the Lord's presence and delivers important messages (Luke 1:19), and Michael, who leads heavenly battles against Satan and God's enemies (Revelation 12:7).

Another prominent angelic figure in the Bible is referred to as "the angel of the Lord." This angel frequently appears in the Old Testament during moments of significant or dramatic intervention. The angel of the Lord primarily acts as God's messenger, preparing the way for God's personal appearance or divine intervention (Exodus 3:2). The angel of the Lord is also mentioned in the New Testament, notably announcing the birth of Jesus to shepherds (Luke 2:9-12) and rolling away the stone at His tomb following the resurrection (Matthew 28:2).

## Types of Angels

### Cherubim
Cherubim are depicted in the Bible as majestic and powerful angelic beings who guard the very presence of God, as well as sacred areas or places of significance. Their primary role involves guarding the holiness of God and protecting access to sacred places or spaces, particularly those that symbolise or represent His presence. Cherubim are first introduced in Genesis 3:24, where

they are depicted guarding the Garden of Eden, preventing humanity's return to the tree of life after Adam and Eve's fall:

*"So he drove out the man; and he placed at the east of the garden of Eden Cherubims, and a flaming sword which turned every way, to keep the way of the tree of life." (Genesis 3:24(NIV))*

These powerful angelic beings are described vividly in Ezekiel's vision, highlighting their majestic presence in God's throne room, symbolising God's holiness and sovereign rule:

*"Then I looked, and behold, in the firmament that was above the head of the cherubims there appeared over them as it were a sapphire stone, as the appearance of the likeness of a throne." (Ezekiel 10:1(NKJV))*

## Seraphim

Seraphim are another distinct group of heavenly beings portrayed as majestic and awe-inspiring. They surround the throne of God, constantly worshipping and praising His holiness and glory. Isaiah offers a vivid description of their appearance and role:

*"Above him were seraphim, each with six wings: With two wings they covered their faces, with two they covered their feet, and with two they were flying. And they were calling to one another: 'Holy, holy, holy is the LORD Almighty; the whole earth is full of his glory.'" (Isaiah 6:2-3(NKJV))*

## Archangels

Archangels hold positions of high authority and command among the angelic host. Michael is explicitly identified as an archangel in Scripture, and he leads angels in spiritual warfare against Satan and his forces. In Revelation 12:7-9, Michael fights victoriously against the dragon (Satan) and his rebellious angels:

*"Then war broke out in heaven. Michael and his angels fought against the dragon, and the dragon and his angels fought back. But he was not strong enough, and they lost their place in heaven. The great dragon was hurled down—that ancient serpent called the devil, or Satan, who leads the whole world astray."*
*(Revelation 12:7-9 (NIV))*

Additionally, in 1 Thessalonians 4:16(NIV), Michael's role is emphasised as central in the dramatic return of Christ:

*"For the Lord himself will come down from heaven, with a loud command, with the voice of the archangel and with the trumpet call of God, and the dead in Christ will rise first."*

### Angels (Messengers)
General angels frequently appear throughout Scripture carrying messages directly from God to humanity. Their primary role is communication—revealing God's intentions, plans, and promises to human beings. A clear example of such angelic visitation is recorded in Luke's Gospel, where Gabriel brings news of the birth of Jesus Christ to Mary:

*"Greetings, you who are highly favoured! The Lord is with you."*
*(Luke 1:28(NKJV))*

### Guardian Angels
Guardian angels are specifically tasked with protecting and guiding individuals throughout their lives. Scripture confirms their existence, demonstrating God's personal and protective care for

humanity. Psalm 91:11 confirms their active role in the life of believers:

*"For he will command his angels concerning you to guard you in all your ways." (Psalm 91:11*(NKJV)*)*

Additionally, Jesus alludes to guardian angels who watch over individuals, particularly children, emphasising their closeness to God:

*"See that you do not despise one of these little ones. For I tell you that their angels in heaven always see the face of my Father in heaven." (Matthew 18:10*(NIV)*)*

**Fallen Angels**

Not all angels have remained faithful to God. Scripture clearly shows that some angels, led by Satan, rebelled against God's authority and were subsequently cast out of heaven. Again, Revelation 12:7-9 illustrates this spiritual rebellion and its outcome, indicating that a significant portion of angels joined Satan in his rebellion.

These fallen angels became spiritual adversaries actively working against God's purposes and His people.

**Angels as Messengers and Protectors of God's People**

Angels frequently appear in the Scriptures with messages from God. One powerful example of this is recorded in Genesis 22:11-18(NKJV):

*"But the angel of the LORD called out to him from heaven,*
*'Abraham! Abraham!'*
*'Here I am,' he replied.*

*'Do not lay a hand on the boy,' he said. 'Do not do anything to him. Now I know that you fear God, because you have not withheld from me your son, your only son.' Abraham looked up and there in a thicket he saw a ram caught by its horns. He went over and took the ram and sacrificed it as a burnt offering instead of his son. So Abraham called that place 'The LORD Will Provide.' And to this day it is said, 'On the mountain of the LORD it will be provided.' The angel of the LORD called to Abraham from heaven a second time and said, 'I swear by myself,' declares the LORD, 'that because you have done this and have not withheld your son, your only son, I will surely bless you and make your descendants as numerous as the stars in the sky and as the sand on the seashore. Your descendants will take possession of the cities of their enemies, and through your offspring all nations on earth will be blessed, because you have obeyed me.'"*

In this passage, the angel of the Lord acted as a messenger, providing critical instruction, encouragement, and reassurance of God's faithfulness and provision.

Angels also have the important role of worshipping and praising God continually. This aspect of their function is beautifully captured in Isaiah 6:2-3[NIV]:

*"Above him were seraphim, each with six wings: With two wings they covered their faces, with two they covered their feet, and with two they were flying. And they were calling to one another: 'Holy, holy, holy is the LORD Almighty; the whole earth is full of his glory.'"*

Here we see angels actively worshipping and honouring God's holiness, continually declaring His majestic glory.

Additionally, angels have the divine assignment of protecting God's people. Psalm 91:11-12[(NIV)] clearly confirms this:

*"For he will command his angels concerning you to guard you in all your ways; they will lift you up in their hands, so that you will not strike your foot against a stone."*

This scripture reveals God's commitment to our safety, promising angelic intervention to protect us from harm, danger, and accidents.

Furthermore, angels are tasked with executing God's righteous judgement, as demonstrated vividly in 2 Kings 19:35[(NJKV)]:

*"That night the angel of the LORD went out and put to death a hundred and eighty-five thousand in the Assyrian camp. When the people got up the next morning—there were all the dead bodies!"*

Through these biblical accounts, we clearly see that God's angels have multiple divine functions and responsibilities, including conveying divine messages, offering constant worship, providing supernatural protection, and carrying out God's judgement. Their protective role, specifically emphasised in Psalm 91:11-12, is an incredible source of comfort and reassurance to us, as God's people.

## 10

# THE LIMITS OF HUMAN AUTHORITY OVER ANGELS

A Biblical Perspective

---

### Do Christians Have Authority to Command Angels?

In recent weeks, I've heard people commanding angels during their prayers and even while preaching. Hearing this made me feel uneasy because I could not recall any scripture supporting this kind of practice. Consequently, I felt it necessary to briefly address this matter from a scriptural perspective to clarify any misunderstandings. To my knowledge, there is no scripture in the Bible where individuals directly command angels to fulfil their personal desires—not even Jesus Christ himself did this.

Therefore, in response to the question, "Do Christians have the authority to command angels?" the answer from scripture is unequivocally "no."

The Bible explicitly teaches that it is God alone who commands His angels concerning us. We do not possess the authority to issue direct orders to angelic beings. Instead, scripture instructs us clearly that we can—and should—pray to God, appealing to Him alone for angelic help. Angels act solely on God's command, not ours.

Matthew 26:53[NKJV]reinforces this point explicitly, stating:

*"Do you think that I cannot appeal to my Father, and he will at once send me more than twelve legions of angels?"*

From this verse, we can clearly see that even Jesus Christ, with all his divinity and humanity, did not command angels directly. Instead, He demonstrated for us how to appeal directly to God the Father, who then releases angels according to His sovereign will and authority.

We also find evidence of this principle in the Old Testament. Moses described an occasion when the children of Israel cried out to God:

*"When we cried out to the LORD, he heard our cry and sent an angel, and brought us out of Egypt"* (Numbers 20:16[NIV]).

This scripture distinctly reveals that the Israelites themselves did not command the angels; rather, they appealed to God, under whose command angels operate.

Furthermore, we must understand the proper hierarchical relationship between humans and angels. Angels are beings of higher rank than humans, as clearly articulated in Hebrews 2:7-9[NIV]:

*"You have made him a little lower than the angels; You have crowned him with glory and honour, and set him over the works of Your hands. You have put all things in subjection under his feet."*

The same point is echoed in Psalm 8:4-5[NKJV]:

*"What is mankind that you are mindful of them, human beings that you care for them? You have made them a little lower than the angels and crowned them with glory and honour."*

Though angels presently occupy a higher rank, scripture tells us that in the future we, as believers, will be entrusted with judging angels, as stated in 1 Corinthians 6:3[NIV]:

*"Do you not know that we will judge angels?"*

It remains essential for us to recognise that angels are spiritual beings, created by God specifically to serve His purposes. We, therefore, have the privilege to appeal in prayer directly to our heavenly Father, through the name of Jesus Christ, to dispatch angels to protect, preserve, provide, and assist us throughout our lives. Nevertheless, it remains firmly established in scripture that we cannot directly command angels, nor should we pray to or worship them.

This principle is explicitly demonstrated when God used an angel to reveal future events to the apostle John. John's immediate reaction was to fall down and worship the angel, but the angel strongly rebuked him:

> *"But he said to me, 'Don't do that! I am a fellow servant with you and with your fellow prophets and with all who keep the words of this scroll. Worship God!'"* (Revelation 22:9(NKJV)).

With these biblical truths clearly in view, let's now explore various examples of individuals who experienced God dispatching His angels to perform extraordinary miracles, delivering them from threats, intimidation, and imminent danger.

# 11

# SUPERNATURAL DELIVERANCE

Biblical Accounts of Divine Protection

---

Throughout the Bible, we see powerful examples of God's supernatural protection over His people. From prison doors miraculously opening to the mouths of lions being shut, these accounts serve as undeniable proof that divine safety is a tangible reality, not just a theological concept.

This chapter explores biblical narratives where individuals faced imminent danger but were delivered by God's mighty hand. Whether through angelic intervention, divine favour, or unwavering faith, these stories reveal that God is always watching over His children, ensuring their protection against the forces of darkness.

As we examine these extraordinary testimonies, let us be reminded that the same God who rescued Peter from prison and Daniel from the lions' den is still at work today. His power is unchanging, and His protection is available to all who trust in Him.

## Individuals That Have Experienced God's Protection:

### The Apostle Peter

Acts 12:1-11<sup>(NKJV)</sup>states: *It was about this time that King Herod arrested some who belonged to the church, intending to persecute them. He had James, the brother of John, put to death with the sword. When he saw that this met with approval among the Jews, he proceeded to seize Peter also. This happened during the Festival of Unleavened Bread. After arresting him, he put him in prison, handing him over to be guarded by four squads of four soldiers each. Herod intended to bring him out for public trial after the Passover.*

*So Peter was kept in prison, but the church was earnestly praying to God for him.*

*The night before Herod was to bring him to trial, Peter was sleeping between two soldiers, bound with two chains, and sentries stood guard at the entrance. Suddenly an angel of the Lord appeared and a light shone in the cell. He struck Peter on the side and woke him up. "Quick, get up!" he said, and the chains fell off Peter's wrists.*

*Then the angel said to him, "Put on your clothes and sandals."
And Peter did so. "Wrap your cloak around you and follow me,"
the angel told him. Peter followed him out of the prison, but he
had no idea that what the angel was doing was really happening;
he thought he was seeing a vision. They passed the first and
second guards and came to the iron gate leading to the city. It
opened for them by itself, and they went through it. When they
had walked the length of one street, suddenly the angel left him.*

*Then Peter came to himself and said, "Now I know without a
doubt that the Lord has sent his angel and rescued me from
Herod's clutches and from everything the Jewish people were
hoping would happen."*

In the passage above, Luke vividly describes for us the miraculous escape Peter experienced from prison through the intervention of an angel sent by God. This detailed account validates that divine safety and protection are not just theoretical ideas or appealing concepts; rather, it proves to us that they are indeed supernatural realities. Peter was faced with the immediate threat and strong possibility of dying in the same manner that the Apostle James had died at the hands of King Herod. The scripture explicitly informs us that when Herod saw the death of James pleased the Jewish people, he deliberately proceeded with capturing Peter as well, fully intending to kill him also. However, the Bible says that the church prayed without ceasing on Peter's behalf, and as a direct result of their fervent prayers, God sent an angel who delivered Peter from Herod's grasp and from the destructive expectations of the Jewish populace.

The church did not passively wait to see what fate would befall Peter. They already knew exactly what the likely outcome would be, given what had tragically happened to James shortly before. So, even amid their intense fear, distress, and grief resulting from the harsh persecution they were enduring, they recognised the opportunity to run swiftly to God in earnest prayer, asking Him to intervene and change the outcome of Peter's desperate situation. I can clearly picture them coming before God filled with fear, distress, uncertainty, and perhaps even a sense of hopelessness due to the severity of the threat they faced. Yet, even amid their troubled emotions and uncertainty, God attentively heard their prayers and intervened powerfully to rescue Peter.

There are several vital insights we can gain from this account, particularly concerning the importance of praying fervently or without ceasing. Scripture clearly reminds us of the effectiveness of earnest prayer, as described by James 5:16[(KJV)], which states explicitly:

*"The effectual fervent prayer of a righteous man availeth much."*

This naturally leads us to the question, "What exactly does it mean to pray fervently or without ceasing?"

According to Bennett, B.[16] (2017), the phrase *'effectual fervent'* comes from one Greek word, ***energeo,*** which means "to be operative, to put forth power, or to effect." In other words, an effectual fervent prayer is one that puts forth power and produces an actual effect or tangible result. Naturally, we might wonder when exactly it is appropriate or necessary to pray such powerful prayers. The biblical example of Elijah provides insight into this. Even though Elijah had already received a clear word from God declaring that it would rain, he did not simply rest upon this promise. Instead, he persisted in fervent prayer, continuing to pray earnestly until he finally saw a small cloud—no larger than the size of a man's hand—appearing in the distant sky.

This demonstrates the principle of effectual fervent prayer, emphasising the necessity of persistence and intentionality in our prayers. When we pray fervently, we engage in a powerful spiritual act, activating the supernatural realm on our behalf. Through such intense and intentional prayers, we are able to access the supernatural help and intervention that God provides, including angelic assistance that God dispatches according to His sovereign will.

Moreover, fervent prayer brings about supernatural deliverance, empowering believers to experience outcomes that override natural circumstances and situations. Such prayer does not merely rely on what we see or feel in the natural realm, but rather presses through into the spiritual, establishing God's will and purposes. In addition to supernatural intervention, praying fervently also releases God's peace into seemingly impossible situations. We see this clearly in Peter's experience: even though he was in prison, bound by chains, and under guard, facing imminent death, he was still able to sleep peacefully, experiencing the divine peace of God despite the dreadful and distressing situation.

Thus, we learn from Elijah's example, as well as Peter's experience, that praying fervently is not just an act of desperation but rather an active partnership with God. It serves to release divine intervention, angelic help, supernatural deliverance, and peace from God in every situation we face.

## Daniel in the Den of Lions

### Daniel 6:1-24<sup>(NIV)</sup>

*"It pleased Darius to appoint 120 satraps to rule throughout the kingdom, with three administrators over them, one of whom was Daniel. The satraps were made accountable to them so that the king might not suffer loss. Now Daniel so distinguished himself among the administrators and the satraps by his exceptional qualities that the king planned to set him over the whole kingdom. At this, the administrators and the satraps tried to find grounds for charges against Daniel in his conduct of government affairs, but they were unable to do so. They could find no corruption in him, because he was trustworthy and neither corrupt nor negligent. Finally these men said, "We will never find any basis for charges against this man Daniel unless it has something to do with the law of his God."*

*So these administrators and satraps went as a group to the king and said: "May King Darius live forever! The royal administrators, prefects, satraps, advisers and governors have all agreed that the king should issue an edict and enforce the decree that anyone who prays to any god or human being during the next thirty days, except to you, Your Majesty, shall be thrown into the lions' den. Now, Your Majesty, issue the decree and put it in writing so that it cannot be altered—in accordance with the*

*law of the Medes and Persians, which cannot be repealed." So
King Darius put the decree in writing.*

*Now when Daniel learned that the decree had been published, he
went home to his upstairs room where the windows opened
toward Jerusalem. Three times a day he got down on his
knees and prayed, giving thanks to his God, just as he had done
before. Then these men went as a group and found Daniel
praying and asking God for help. So they went to the king and
spoke to him about his royal decree: "Did you not publish a
decree that during the next thirty days anyone who prays to any
god or human being except to you, Your Majesty, would be
thrown into the lions' den?"*

*The king answered, "The decree stands—in accordance with the
law of the Medes and Persians, which cannot be repealed."*

*Then they said to the king, "Daniel, who is one of the exiles from
Judah, pays no attention to you, Your Majesty, or to the decree
you put in writing. He still prays three times a day." When the
king heard this, he was greatly distressed; he was determined to
rescue Daniel and made every effort until sundown to save him.*

*Then the men went as a group to King Darius and said to him,
"Remember, Your Majesty, that according to the law of the
Medes and Persians no decree or edict that the king issues can be
changed."*

So the king gave the order, and they brought Daniel and threw him into the lions' den. The king said to Daniel, "May your God, whom you serve continually, rescue you!"

A stone was brought and placed over the mouth of the den, and the king sealed it with his own signet ring and with the rings of his nobles, so that Daniel's situation might not be changed. [18] Then the king returned to his palace and spent the night without eating and without any entertainment being brought to him. And he could not sleep.

At the first light of dawn, the king got up and hurried to the lions' den. [20] When he came near the den, he called to Daniel in an anguished voice, "Daniel, servant of the living God, has your God, whom you serve continually, been able to rescue you from the lions?"

Daniel answered, "May the king live forever! [22] My God sent his angel, and he shut the mouths of the lions. They have not hurt me, because I was found innocent in his sight. Nor have I ever done any wrong before you, Your Majesty."

The king was overjoyed and gave orders to lift Daniel out of the den. And when Daniel was lifted from the den, no wound was found on him, because he had trusted in his God.

At the king's command, the men who had falsely accused Daniel were brought in and thrown into the lions' den, along with their wives and children. And before they reached the floor of the den, the lions overpowered them and crushed all their bones.

When a trap was deliberately set for Daniel, he continued steadfastly in prayer without ceasing, choosing to pray three times each day and consistently giving thanks to his God, rather than praying to or worshipping any human being. Despite knowing the severe consequences that awaited him, Daniel's faithfulness and dedication to God remained unwavering.

Consequently, Daniel was thrown into the lions' den, and the king, greatly distressed by this decision, found himself unable to sleep throughout the night. He anxiously awaited the first signs of dawn, deeply troubled and convinced that the lions would surely devour Daniel. However, when morning finally came, the king rushed immediately to the lions' den and discovered, to his amazement, that Daniel was unharmed. Daniel confidently replied to the king, declaring, "My God sent his angel, and he shut the mouths of the lions" (Daniel 6:22$^{(NIV)}$).

This remarkable event demonstrates clearly that supernatural safety and divine protection are genuine and tangible realities. They are not mere figments of our imagination or fantasies conjured up to give false hope; instead, they are authentic spiritual experiences that can, will, and indeed are being encountered by many believers here and now in their everyday lives.

Perhaps, as you are reading this right now, you might find yourself feeling deeply fearful or anxious due to the disturbing scenes of violence, tragedy, or danger you have witnessed either on social media, television, or even personally. My earnest prayer and desire for you at this very moment is that God Almighty would release His angel—or even multiple angels—to minister healing, deliverance, comfort, and supernatural protection to you in your current situation. May the same powerful God who supernaturally shut the mouths of the lions to protect Daniel from harm, do exactly the same for you today, providing you with divine safety and shelter from danger.

Supernatural safety and divine protection are your covenant right and inheritance through Jesus Christ. If we fail to wholeheartedly accept and embrace the reality of this supernatural protection made available through God's precious Son, Jesus Christ, we run the risk of becoming vulnerable and falling victim to the various evils and dangers prevalent in this present world. It is therefore crucial that we consciously acknowledge and affirm this divine reality, continually standing firm in our faith and reliance upon God's unfailing promises of safety and protection.

# 12

# DIVINE PRESERVATION

God's Supernatural Protection Through the Ages

---

From the earliest biblical accounts to the life of Jesus Christ and beyond, God's supernatural preservation has remained a central theme of His divine nature. Whether through angelic warnings, miraculous deliverances, or direct intervention, God has continually shielded His people from harm, ensuring that His purpose prevails.

This chapter explores remarkable instances of divine preservation, demonstrating how God's protective hand guided and secured His chosen ones. From the flight of Jesus into Egypt to Moses leading the Israelites through the Red Sea, we see clear evidence that God's preservation is not limited by time or circumstance.

As you read, may these testimonies inspire faith, deepen trust in God's sovereignty, and reassure you that His protective power is still at work in our lives today. His promises remain steadfast: He is our refuge, our shield, and our ever-present help in times of trouble.

## Jesus Christ and God's Divine Preservation:

### Matthew 2:11-15<sup>(NKJV)</sup>

*And when they had come into the house, they saw the young Child with Mary His mother, and fell down and worshiped Him. And when they had opened their treasures, they presented gifts to Him: gold, frankincense, and myrrh.*

*Then, being divinely warned in a dream that they should not return to Herod, they departed for their own country another way.*

### The Flight into Egypt

*Now when they had departed, behold, an angel of the Lord appeared to Joseph in a dream, saying, "Arise, take the young Child and His mother, flee to Egypt, and stay there until I bring you word; for Herod will seek the young Child to destroy Him."*

*When he arose, he took the young Child and His mother by night and departed for Egypt, and was there until the death of Herod, that it might be fulfilled which was spoken by the Lord through the prophet, saying, "Out of Egypt I called My Son."*

In this passage of Scripture, we can clearly observe how God, in His great mercy, foresight, and wisdom, provided divine protection and preservation for Jesus Christ when He was still a baby. At the time, Herod was intent on killing the child who was prophesied to be king, viewing Jesus as a threat to his reign and authority. To thwart Herod's plans, God first communicated to the wise men through a dream, warning them not to return to Herod as previously instructed, but rather to return to their country by another route. This divine intervention ensured that Herod would not gain knowledge about the child's exact whereabouts.

Following the departure of the wise men, God also spoke directly to Joseph in a dream, instructing him to urgently flee with Mary and the young child to Egypt, and remain there until further instruction was provided. Joseph immediately acted upon this divine guidance, swiftly leaving with his family under the cover of night to ensure their safety and security. This decisive and prompt obedience exemplifies genuine faith, accompanied by wisdom in action. Joseph's faith did not lead him to passively wait and see what might happen; instead, it compelled him to heed God's instruction immediately and take necessary precautions to protect his family.

Proverbs 22:3[(NIV)] supports this principle clearly, declaring, *"The prudent see danger and take refuge, but the simple keep going and pay the penalty."* This verse powerfully highlights the necessity for wisdom alongside our faith, indicating that true and biblical faith includes prudent discernment and appropriate action when faced with imminent danger. True faith given by God always possesses wisdom, as wisdom is intrinsically woven into the very nature of faith itself, because it originates from an all-knowing and all-wise God.

Therefore, even as we wholeheartedly believe in God's supernatural protection, we must also recognise our responsibility to put into place all necessary natural safety measures. Whether it concerns our personal safety, homes, businesses, communities, or families, we should diligently ensure that we are actively safeguarding ourselves to the best of our abilities. Faith in God's divine hand of protection must always be accompanied by wise practical steps, for God-given faith does not exclude wisdom, but rather fully embraces and operates through it.

## Moses and the nation of Israel

*Exodus 13:14-31(NIV)*
*Moses answered the people, "Do not be afraid. Stand firm and you will see the deliverance the Lord will bring you today. The Egyptians you see today you will never see again. The Lord will fight for you; you need only to be still."*

*Then the Lord said to Moses, "Why are you crying out to me? Tell the Israelites to move on. Raise your staff and stretch out your hand over the sea to divide the water so that the Israelites can go through the sea on dry ground. I will harden the hearts of the Egyptians so that they will go in after them. And I will gain glory through Pharaoh and all his army, through his chariots and his horsemen. The Egyptians will know that I am the Lord when I gain glory through Pharaoh, his chariots and his horsemen."*

*Then the angel of God, who had been traveling in front of Israel's army, withdrew and went behind them. The pillar of cloud also moved from in front and stood behind them, coming between the armies of Egypt and Israel. Throughout the night the cloud brought darkness to the one side and light to the other side; so neither went near the other all night long.*

*Then Moses stretched out his hand over the sea, and all that night the Lord drove the sea back with a strong east wind and turned it into dry land. The waters were divided, and the Israelites went through the sea on dry ground, with a wall of water on their right and on their left.*

*The Egyptians pursued them, and all Pharaoh's horses and chariots and horsemen followed them into the sea. During the last watch of the night the Lord looked down from the pillar of fire and cloud at the Egyptian army and threw it into confusion. He jammed the wheels of their chariots so that they had difficulty driving. And the Egyptians said, "Let's get away from the Israelites! The Lord is fighting for them against Egypt."*

*Then the Lord said to Moses, "Stretch out your hand over the sea so that the waters may flow back over the Egyptians and their chariots and horsemen." Moses stretched out his hand over the sea, and at daybreak the sea went back to its place. The Egyptians were fleeing toward it, and the Lord swept them into the sea. The water flowed back and covered the chariots and horsemen—the entire army of Pharaoh that had followed the Israelites into the sea. Not one of them survived.*

*But the Israelites went through the sea on dry ground, with a wall of water on their right and on their left. That day the Lord saved Israel from the hands of the Egyptians, and Israel saw the Egyptians lying dead on the shore. And when the Israelites saw the mighty hand of the Lord displayed against the Egyptians, the people feared the Lord and put their trust in him and in Moses his servant."*

The Lord hardened Pharaoh's heart after he had decided to let the Israelites go. As a result, Pharaoh changed his mind and chose to pursue them, intending to capture and enslave them once again. This decision is clearly illustrated in Exodus 14:5$^{(NIV)}$, which says, *"When the king of Egypt was told that the people had fled, Pharaoh and his officials changed their minds about them and said, 'What have we done? We have let the Israelites go and have lost their services!'"* Driven by this intention, Pharaoh assembled his armies and chased after them.

In response, God demonstrated His supernatural power and protection. He intervened miraculously, ensuring that Pharaoh's plan was ultimately frustrated and defeated. As Pharaoh and his army pursued the Israelites, God threw their plans into confusion. He caused the wheels of their chariots to come off and obstructed their progress so that they could not reach the Israelites. This led to their complete defeat at the Red Sea.

To you who are reading this right now, my prayer and heartfelt declaration is that the Lord would do the very same for you. May every enemy attempting to sabotage your purpose, destiny, and peace be utterly disappointed and confounded in their efforts to bring harm, injury, or danger to you and your family, in the mighty name of Jesus Christ. May God cause confusion among those who pursue you, dismantling every strategy, method, and vehicle used to hinder your progress and steal your peace.

The Word of the Lord declares in Psalm 91:7$^{(NIV)}$ "*A thousand may fall at your side, ten thousand at your right hand, but it will not come near you.*" Verse 8 further states, "*You will only observe with your eyes and see the punishment of the wicked.*" Such divine safety and protection are guaranteed for those who genuinely make the Lord their refuge and hiding place.

Praise God that you and I have been set apart and preserved by Him for such a time as this, to declare His unwavering goodness and mercy. Even in moments when it may feel difficult to sense His presence—especially in times of struggle, threat, or danger—His promise remains steadfast and true: "He will never leave us nor forsake us."

Yes, it is true that at certain times we may feel as though God is distant, particularly when life's challenges, hardships, or threats confront us. Yet, these feelings do not reflect reality, as evidenced by numerous biblical accounts of God's unwavering protection and preservation in the lives of so many individuals, including Jesus Christ Himself. Though Satan intended evil for these people, God's great mercy, wisdom, and faithfulness turned each situation around, bringing about good from what was meant for harm. This same God continues to watch over us, ensuring our protection and preservation in every situation we face. Hallelujah!

Romans 8:28$^{(KJV)}$ states, "*And we know that all things work together for good to them that love God, to them who are the called according to his purpose.*" This scripture reassures us that God, in His infinite wisdom and mercy, will ensure that every circumstance—no matter how difficult, troubling, or distressing—will ultimately work for our good, as we place our love and trust in Him. This does not imply that everything we experience is inherently good; rather, it emphasises that our sovereign God is able to take even negative, harmful, and troubling circumstances and use them for our ultimate benefit and His glory.

Ephesians 2:8-9[(NIV)] reminds us clearly that our protection, preservation, and salvation are a result of God's grace and not our own works: "*For it is by grace you have been saved, through faith—and this is not from yourselves, it is the gift of God—not by works, so that no one can boast.*" This serves as a comforting reminder that we do not earn supernatural protection or deliverance through personal efforts or merit, but rather, it comes solely as an undeserved gift from a loving Father. God's supernatural protection and safety are freely given out of His boundless love and kindness towards us.

The powerful and supernatural deliverances we have examined earlier—from Daniel's protection in the lions' den, to Peter's miraculous prison escape, and even the preservation of baby Jesus—clearly demonstrate that our heavenly Father will indeed use every available means, natural or supernatural, angelic or otherwise, to ensure our safety. These extraordinary encounters reveal the depth of God's unwavering commitment to the well-being and safety of His children, highlighting His willingness and ability to step into our natural circumstances with His supernatural power.

# I DECREE AND DECLARE

I decree and declare that the same Almighty God who faithfully protected Daniel in the lions' den, delivered Peter from imprisonment, and preserved the life of Jesus as a child, will surely protect me and my entire household. The hand of God safeguards my family, my spouse, children, grandchildren, my business, career, finances, health, ministry, and possessions. As declared in **Isaiah 54:17**, no weapon forged against me shall prosper.

I speak forth Psalm 35:8[(NKJV)], *"Let destruction come upon my enemy by surprise; let the very net hidden for me catch him, and let him fall into his own destruction!"* Every weapon, scheme, or evil intention set up against me shall fail, for God Almighty is my defence and my protector. May every curse, evil incantation, and negative word uttered by witches, warlocks, or any forces of darkness against my life be destroyed right now by the consuming fire of the Holy Spirit.

I declare according to **Psalm 91:11**[(NIV)], *"He will command his angels concerning you to guard you in all your ways."* Lord, release your angels to shield me and guide me safely through every moment and season of life. Heavenly Father, you are my rock, my fortress, and my hiding place. Let every trap set by the enemy become his own downfall. Let your divine fire consume and dismantle every plan of wickedness fashioned for my downfall. You alone, God, are my refuge and stronghold in every circumstance, and I confidently rest in your supernatural protection, in the mighty name of Jesus Christ!

## 13

# UNMASKING THE ENEMY

Understanding Satan's Nature and Strategies

---

Satan's destructive agenda is evident all around us—his tactics are designed to steal, kill, and destroy every aspect of our lives. Yet, as believers, we are not left powerless. Through Christ, we have been equipped with divine authority to resist and overcome his schemes.

This chapter delves into the nature of Satan, exposing his character, strategies, and the spiritual warfare he wages against humanity. By understanding his methods—deception, accusation, and manipulation—we can stand firm against his attacks and walk in the victory Christ has already secured for us.

As you read, may your spiritual discernment sharpen, your faith be strengthened, and your confidence in God's ultimate authority over the enemy grow unwavering.

Looking around us each day, we can clearly see that the enemy is constantly seeking opportunities to destroy, steal, and kill. Everywhere we turn, evidence of his destructive nature is painfully apparent. It is an undeniable reality that Satan cannot alter or change his nature. He is out twenty-four hours a day, seven days a week, continually moving around with his cohorts, who are demons, actively destroying, stealing, and killing.

He is relentless and is constantly after our families, marriages, children, finances, careers, relationships, community, country, businesses, mental health, and physical health. When he succeeds in attacking any of these critical areas, our lives become negatively impacted in many different ways. In some instances, our peace gets severely disrupted, and our joy and health become affected. Some beautiful, lovely, and peaceful homes have been destroyed, marriages have fallen apart, and children have been scattered and left vulnerable. We have witnessed people losing their jobs unfairly, causing them severe financial distress, hardship, anxiety, and deep depression.

As a result of these vicious attacks from Satan, we have seen an increase in domestic and gender-based violence within our homes, our communities, and even throughout our country. Signs of broken relationships amongst families, friends, neighbours, and co-workers have become increasingly evident as we gaze around and witness wickedness openly displayed.

However, despite this troubling reality, we thank God for Jesus, who came to give us hope and deliverance. He says in His Word, "I have come that they may have life and have it to the full." It is because of His coming that we can no longer just sit down, relax, or passively accept all the visible signs of Satan's destructive nature together with his demons. Instead, we can boldly and confidently take a firm stand of faith and begin to pray earnestly. We can call upon the mighty name of the Lord Jesus to intervene, to halt and put an end to all of Satan's stealing, destroying, killing, and deception.

We must always bear in mind that Satan himself cannot change or alter his destructive nature, which is to steal, kill, and destroy. Nevertheless, through the extraordinary power of the blood of Jesus Christ, we, as believers, have the authority to disrupt, dismantle, and completely frustrate his plans, preventing him from successfully carrying out his damaging operations.

Ezekiel 28:14–16[NIV] states the following about Satan:
"You were the anointed cherub who covers;
I established you;
You were on the holy mountain of God;
You walked back and forth in the midst of fiery stones.
You were perfect in your ways from the day you were created,
Till iniquity was found in you.
By the abundance of your trading
You became filled with violence within,
And you sinned;
Therefore, I cast you as a profane thing
Out of the mountain of God;

> And I destroyed you, O covering cherub,
> From the midst of the fiery stones."

Satan was indeed the first to harbour the attitude and intention of murder, and he has consistently promoted this destructive attitude ever since. According to Martin G. Collins[17], *"A murderer is a child of Satan with the same arrogant pride. Such a person will not enter God's Kingdom"*

This insight from Collins highlights the serious consequences tied to the attitude of murder, clearly illustrating how it aligns with Satan's original nature and prideful arrogance, which resulted in his own downfall. It is crucial to recognise this critical reality, as it empowers us, as believers, to remain vigilant and alert, understanding clearly that Satan's intentions are consistently centred on causing destruction, harm, and death. Therefore, by comprehending this fundamental truth, we are better positioned spiritually to resist Satan's tactics effectively.

His relentless pursuit is aimed at creating situations that result in suffering, conflict, and destruction in our lives, families, communities, and the world at large. However, with this awareness and understanding firmly in mind, we are strengthened and encouraged as believers to stand boldly in our faith, to pray with fervency, and to confidently invoke the power and presence of Jesus Christ. Christ came specifically to bring abundant life, healing, deliverance, and freedom from Satan's destructive influence. This allows us, as children of God, to confidently assert the promises and blessings of life, healing, and deliverance that Christ secured for us through His sacrifice.

Galatians 5:21(NKJV)warns us explicitly of the consequences of indulging in sinful behaviours, stating: *"Envy, murders, drunkenness, revelries, and the like; of which I tell you beforehand, just as I also told you in time past, that those who practice such things will not inherit the kingdom of God."* This verse serves as a powerful reminder that those who align themselves with such actions are operating outside of God's will and are in danger of being separated from His kingdom.

Similarly, 1 John 3:15(NKJV)reinforces the seriousness of harbouring hatred, equating it to murder: *"Whoever hates his brother is a murderer, and you know that no murderer has eternal life abiding in him."* This verse highlights the profound spiritual implications of allowing hatred to take root in one's heart. According to Scripture, hatred is not merely an emotion but an active alignment with Satan's destructive nature. To hate is to murder in the heart, demonstrating a character opposed to the love and righteousness of God.

These scriptures further illustrate the true nature of Satan's influence in the world and the traits that define his character. He is the origin of envy, malice, deception, and destruction, manifesting his wickedness in those who yield to his temptations. His attributes stand in stark contrast to the fruit of the Spirit, which reflects God's divine nature. Understanding this contrast is essential for every believer, as it helps us discern the tactics of the enemy and resist the sinful tendencies he promotes.

Satan's character is rooted in deception, pride, and rebellion against God. His nature is explicitly revealed through Scripture,

119

exposing his evil and corrupt character. His tactics are designed to corrupt, tempt, and ultimately separate individuals from God's presence. Through these biblical warnings, we are reminded to guard our hearts, reject the works of the enemy, and walk in the light of God's truth, fully embracing the life and protection found in Jesus Christ.

These passages provide a clear understanding of his attributes, illustrating the extent of his wickedness and his unrelenting opposition to God's truth and righteousness.

Firstly, he is described as a **murderer and a liar.** In *John* 8:44[(NIV)], Jesus Himself confronts the Pharisees, stating: *"You are of your father the devil, and your will is to do your father's desires. He was a murderer from the beginning and does not stand in the truth because there is no truth in him. When he lies, he speaks out of his own character, for he is a liar and the father of lies."* This verse makes it abundantly clear that deception and destruction are at the very core of Satan's nature. From the very beginning, he sought to corrupt, deceive, and ultimately bring death upon humanity. His lies led to the fall of man, and he continues to operate as the father of lies, using deception as his primary weapon to lead people away from God.

Secondly, Satan is called a **sinner.** *1 John 3:7-10*[(NIV)] states: *"Little children, let no one deceive you. Whoever practices righteousness is righteous, as he is righteous. Whoever makes a practice of sinning is of the devil, for the devil has been sinning from the beginning. The reason the Son of God appeared was to destroy the works of the devil. No one born of God makes a practice of* *sinning, for God's seed abides in him; and he cannot keep on sinning because he has been born of God. By this, it is evident who are the children of God, and who are the children of the devil: whoever does not practice righteousness is not of God, nor is the one who does not love his brother."*

Satan is the very essence of sin, having sinned from the beginning and continuously leading others into rebellion against God. This passage also highlights the distinction between the children of God and the children of the devil—those who persist in sin and refuse to walk in righteousness are following the nature of Satan.

Furthermore, Scripture identifies Satan as an *accuser. Zechariah 3:1-4*(NIV) illustrates this when it states: *"Then he showed me Joshua the high priest standing before the angel of the LORD, and Satan standing at his right hand to accuse him. And the LORD said to Satan, 'The LORD rebuke you, O Satan! The LORD who has chosen Jerusalem rebuke you! Is not this a brand plucked from the fire?' Now Joshua was standing before the angel, clothed with filthy garments. And the angel said to those who were standing before him, 'Remove the filthy garments from him.' And to him, he said, 'Behold, I have taken your iniquity away from you, and I will clothe you with pure vestments.'"*

Satan is relentless in bringing accusations against believers, seeking to condemn them before God. Yet, the Lord Himself rebukes him, demonstrating that God's mercy and righteousness always triumph over the enemy's accusations.

Satan is also revealed as a *deceiver. Revelation 20:10*(NKJV)declares: *"And the devil who had deceived them was thrown into the lake of fire and sulfur where the beast and the false prophet were, and they will be tormented day and night forever and ever.*" His mission is to mislead, trick, and confuse, distorting the truth to keep people enslaved in sin. His deception is the primary reason why so many reject the Gospel, choosing instead to follow the lies he has planted in the world.

Additionally, he is called a ***thief***. *John 10:10*<sup>(NIV)</sup> states: *"The thief comes only to steal and kill and destroy; I have come that they may have life and have it to the full."* Satan operates through theft, not only in the physical sense but also in the spiritual. He seeks to steal joy, peace, hope, and faith, keeping people bound in fear, doubt, and oppression.

Moreover, Scripture warns us that Satan is a ***disguiser***. *2 Corinthians 11:14*<sup>(NIV)</sup> says: *"No wonder, for even Satan disguises himself as an angel of light."*

He masquerades as something good, appearing as light when, in reality, he is the embodiment of darkness. This is why discernment through the Holy Spirit is crucial, as Satan manipulates and deceives under the guise of righteousness.

These characteristics confirm that Satan is wholly evil, diabolical, and a traitor of the highest degree. He will never change, as his fate has already been sealed by God. His ultimate destiny is eternal judgment, and every scheme he devises will ultimately fail before the power and sovereignty of God.

As believers, understanding the true nature of Satan equips us to stand firm in faith, resist his deceptions, and embrace the victorious power of Jesus Christ. Through Christ, we overcome every lie, accusation, and attack of the enemy, walking in divine protection, truth, and victory.

# 14

# THE ULTIMATE PASSOVER

Jesus' Blood, Redemption, and Divine Protection

---

Throughout history, God has provided powerful symbols and prophetic foreshadowing of His divine plan for redemption and protection. One of the most significant events in biblical history—the first Passover—served as a striking preview of a greater, eternal reality that would later be fulfilled through Jesus Christ. This chapter explores the profound connection between the Old Testament Passover and the ultimate sacrifice of Christ, revealing how His death and resurrection secured not only our salvation but also our supernatural safety and divine covering. As we journey through this chapter, we will uncover the depth of God's plan and the lasting impact of Christ's finished work for all who believe.

## The First Passover

The first Passover serves as a typology, a prophetic foreshadowing of the redemptive work of Christ, which was to come.

Exodus 12-1-12[BSV]

*"Now the LORD said to Moses and Aaron in the land of Egypt, "This month is the beginning of months for you; it shall be the first month of your year.*

*Tell the whole congregation of Israel that on the tenth day of this month each man must select a lamb for his family, one per household. If the household is too small for a whole lamb, they are to share with the nearest neighbor based on the number of people, and apportion the lamb accordingly.*

*Your lamb must be an unblemished year-old male, and you may take it from the sheep or the goats. You must keep it until the fourteenth day of the month, when the whole assembly of the congregation of Israel will slaughter the animals at twilight. They are to take some of the blood and put it on the sides and tops of the doorframes of the houses where they eat the lambs.*

*They are to eat the meat that night, roasted over the fire, along with unleavened bread and bitter herbs.*

*Do not eat any of the meat raw or cooked in boiling water, but only roasted over the fire—its head and legs and inner parts. Do not leave any of it until morning; before the morning you must burn up any part that is left over.*

*This is how you are to eat it: You must be fully dressed for travel, with your sandals on your feet and your staff in your hand. You are to eat in haste; it is the LORD's Passover.*

*On that night I will pass through the land of Egypt and strike down every firstborn male, both man and beast, and I will execute judgment against all the gods of Egypt. I am the LORD. The blood on the houses where you are staying will be a sign; when I see the blood, I will pass over you. No plague will fall on you to destroy you when I strike the land of Egypt."*

This scripture provides us with a vivid and detailed account of the specific instructions the Israelites had to follow in order to experience God's supernatural safety, protection, and preservation. The entire congregation of Israel was commanded to apply the blood of an unblemished lamb to the sides and top of their doorframes. This act served as a divine safeguard against the angel of death sent to execute God's judgment upon Egypt.

The way in which the blood was applied symbolically formed the shape of a cross, a prophetic foreshadowing of what was to come—the ultimate sacrifice of Jesus Christ. The blood of the lamb established a clear distinction between the Israelites and the Egyptians. God's instruction was explicit: "*When I see the blood, I will pass over you. No plague will fall on you to destroy you when I strike Egypt.*" (*Exodus 12:13*[NIV]). This divine protection was not based on their nationality, their status, or their works, but solely on the presence of the blood.

The absence of the lamb's blood resulted in devastation for those who failed to apply it, bringing about the death of the firstborn in every Egyptian household. However, for those who obediently followed God's instruction and applied the blood of the unblemished lamb, safety and preservation were guaranteed.

If the blood of a mere animal, under the old covenant, was powerful enough to shield an entire nation from destruction, how much greater is the power of the precious blood of Jesus Christ?

## The Second and Final Passover

Jesus is often referred to as the *Passover Lamb of God*, a title that reflects His role as the ultimate sacrifice for humanity. The Apostle Paul affirms this truth in *1 Corinthians 5:7*[(KJV)]: *"Cleanse out the old leaven that you may be a new lump, as you really are unleavened. For Christ, our Passover lamb, has been sacrificed."* This statement draws a direct parallel between the first Passover in Egypt and the redemptive work of Christ, showing that He is the fulfilment of what was foreshadowed in the Old Testament.

The prophet Isaiah also speaks of Christ's suffering, likening Him to a sacrificial lamb: *"He was oppressed and afflicted, yet he did not open his mouth; he was led like a lamb to the slaughter, and as a sheep before its shearers is silent, so he did not open his mouth"* (*Isaiah 53:7*[(NKJV)]). This prophecy vividly portrays the humility and submission with which Jesus endured suffering and death for the salvation of mankind.

John the Baptist, upon seeing Jesus, declares: *"Look, the Lamb of God, who takes away the sin of the world!"* (*John 1:29*[NIV]). This bold proclamation recognises Jesus as the final and ultimate sacrificial Lamb, the one who came to provide a permanent solution to sin, unlike the temporary sacrifices offered under the Old Covenant.

The fulfilment of what was foreshadowed through the Israelites' exodus from Egypt is fully realised in the death and resurrection of Jesus Christ. The Apostle Paul confirms this in *2 Corinthians 5:21*[NIV]: *"God made him who had no sin to be sin for us, so that in him we might become the righteousness of God."* This divine exchange—where Christ bore our sins so that we could receive His righteousness—is the foundation of our redemption.

Unlike the Old Testament system that required continual sacrifices, Jesus' blood provided eternal redemption. *Hebrews 9:12*[NKJV]states: *"He did not enter by means of the blood of goats and calves; but he entered the Most Holy Place once for all by his own blood, thus obtaining eternal redemption."* His blood, shed on the cross, does not merely cover momentary judgment—it provides *eternal* redemption, *absolute security,* and *supernatural protection* for all who put their trust in Him. His sacrifice was not just a *covering* for sin but a complete and final atonement that reconciled humanity with God.

Because Jesus has already paid the price with His own blood, there is no longer any need for animal sacrifices or the use of animal blood as a covering for protection from death, evil, or natural disasters. The first Passover in *Exodus 12* was a mere shadow of what was to come—a prophetic foreshadowing of Christ's ultimate sacrifice.

The Greek word for *salvation* is *soteria*[18], which encompasses deliverance from both physical danger and the effects of sin. Through Jesus Christ, believers have the power to apply His blood in prayer, declaring the promises of God's Word over their lives, families, marriages, children, communities, careers, and businesses. This divine protection, safety, and preservation are made available to us under the New Covenant, secured by the finished work of Christ.

Through Jesus, a new and better covenant has been established—one that is eternal, unshakable, and far superior to the old. This new template, sealed with His blood, grants believers access to divine security, ensuring that they remain covered under His unfailing grace.

This divine truth remains unshakable: the blood of Jesus marks those who belong to Him, setting them apart and shielding them from the destruction that befalls the world. It is not merely a theological concept but a supernatural reality that every believer can walk in. Through faith in His sacrifice, we are divinely protected, preserved, and set apart for God's glorious purpose.

## The Last Supper Before His Death

During His final meal with His disciples, Jesus instituted what we now call the Lord's Supper or Holy Communion, marking the establishment of the New Covenant in His blood. In *Luke 22:19-20*[NKJV], it is written: *"And He took the bread, gave thanks and broke it, and gave it to them, saying, 'This is My body, given for you; do this in remembrance of Me.' In the same way, after supper He took the cup, saying, 'This cup is the new covenant in My blood, which is poured out for you.'"*

As often as we come together with family, friends, or within the body of Christ, we can partake in Holy Communion, not as a mere ritual, but in remembrance of what Jesus Christ accomplished once and for all. By doing so, we proclaim the power of His sacrifice over our lives and align ourselves with the reality of His divine protection, provision, and redemptive work. Communion is not just symbolic; it is a declaration of our faith in the finished work of the cross and a reassurance that we will experience His visible hand in every area of our lives.

Through His blood, Jesus established a clear distinction between His people and the world, just as the blood of the unblemished lamb distinguished the Israelites from the Egyptians during the first Passover. Yet, Christ's blood is far greater than that of the sacrificial lamb under the Old Covenant. Everything that humanity will ever need—supernatural safety, divine protection, healing, forgiveness, provision, redemption, and justification—is found in the precious, unblemished blood of Jesus Christ.

He is not merely a historical figure who once lived and died; He is *alive* and remains our *living hope*. His resurrection ensures that just as He was raised from the dead, so will we be raised to eternal life. *1 Peter 1:3*[NIV] declares: *"Blessed be the God and Father of our Lord Jesus Christ! According to His great mercy, He has caused us to be born again to a living hope through the resurrection of Jesus Christ from the dead."*

His death and resurrection transformed supernatural safety and divine protection from a mere concept into a reality—one that is accessible to everyone who believes. Those who trust in Him are covered, shielded, and preserved, not only in this life but for eternity. His blood is more than enough, securing our salvation and making us victorious over every scheme of the enemy.

# 15

# THE DIVINE DESIGN OF MAN

Spirit, Soul, and Body

---

Understanding the nature of our being is essential for living in alignment with God's will and experiencing His supernatural safety, healing, and restoration. The Bible reveals that mankind was created as a triune being—spirit, soul, and body—each part playing a unique role in our relationship with God, our personal growth, and our overall well-being. This chapter explores the distinct functions of the spirit, soul, and body, unveiling their significance in our daily walk with Christ and the impact they have on our faith, emotions, and physical health.

*1 Thessalonians 5:23*[(NIV)] *– "May God himself, the God of peace, sanctify you through and through. May your whole spirit, soul* *and body be kept blameless at the coming of our Lord Jesus Christ."*

Having a fundamental understanding of the distinction between the spirit, soul, and body, as outlined in Scripture, is crucial for dealing with each aspect of our being effectively. The Apostle Paul, under divine inspiration, refers to man as a triune being—one person made up of three primary components: spirit, soul, and body. Examining these briefly will provide clarity as we continue through this chapter.

## Man is Spirit

*Genesis 1:26*[KJV] declares: *"And God said, Let us make man in our image, after our likeness: and let them have dominion over the fish of the sea, and over the fowl of the air, and over the cattle, and over all the earth, and over every creeping thing that creepeth upon the earth."*

This passage establishes that humanity was created in the image and likeness of God. Since God is Spirit, it follows that the essence of man is also spirit. This truth is reinforced in *John 4:24*[NIV], which states: *"God is a Spirit: and they that worship him must worship him in spirit and in truth."*

The term *man* here is a generic reference to all of humanity, encompassing both male and female. The spirit is the eternal part of man, the innermost being, which allows for communion and fellowship with God. *Job 32:8*[KJV] further confirms this by stating: *"But there is a spirit in man: and the inspiration of the Almighty giveth them understanding."* This indicates that the spirit within man is the channel through which divine wisdom and revelation flow.

At the time of physical death, Scripture affirms that the spirit of man returns to God. *Ecclesiastes 12:7*(NKJV) states: *"Then the dust will return to the earth as it was, and the spirit will return to God who gave it."* This underscores the temporary nature of the physical body while affirming the eternal existence of the spirit. The spirit is the part of man that is directly connected to God and is the true essence of who we are.

## The Soul

The soul of man consists of the mind, will, and emotions. It is the centre where information is processed, stored, and recalled, much like a computer hard drive. The soul is deeply affected by life experiences, shaping thoughts, decisions, and emotional responses.

*Proverbs 2:10*(NIV) states: *"For wisdom will enter your heart, and knowledge will be pleasant to your soul."*

Each aspect of the soul plays a crucial role in how we interact with the world, how we respond to challenges, and how we align ourselves with God's will.

## The Will

The will is the faculty of choice, determining the actions and decisions we take. Scripture illustrates how the soul exercises the will in moments of choice and rejection.

*Job 6:7*(NKJV)*— "My soul refuses to touch them; They are like loathsome food to me."*

*Job 7:15*(NKJV)*— "So that my soul would choose suffocation, Death rather than my pains."*

These verses demonstrate how the soul has the capacity to reject, refuse, or choose based on conviction, experience, or emotional state.

## Emotions

Emotions are deeply embedded within the soul, influencing how we feel and react to situations. When we go through trials, trauma, and disappointments, our emotions are impacted, leaving behind wounds and scars.

*Job 9:21*(NIV)* — "I am guiltless; I do not take notice of myself; I despise my life."*

*Job 10:1*(NKJV)*— "I loathe my own life; I will give full vent to my complaint; I will speak in the bitterness of my soul."*

These passages illustrate how pain, sorrow, and distress can manifest in deep emotional suffering, sometimes leading to despair, bitterness, and frustration.

## The Mind

The mind is the seat of thought, reasoning, and meditation. It is where knowledge, understanding, and reflection take place.

*Psalm 94:19*(NKJV)*– "When my anxious thoughts multiply within me, your consolations delight my soul."*

*Psalm 119:167*(NKJV)*– "My soul keeps your testimonies, And I love them exceedingly."*

The mind is where thoughts of peace, fear, joy, or anxiety are processed. It is where strongholds can form if we do not align our thoughts with God's truth. This is why renewing the mind is essential for spiritual transformation and healing.

The soul, being the seat of emotions, thoughts, and decisions, is the area that is most affected when we experience pain, disappointment, or trauma. It carries the scars of hijackings, robberies, accidents, bereavement, and other painful experiences, often making it difficult for people to live free from fear, bitterness, anger, hatred, resentment, and unanswered questions.

## The Body

The physical body is the vessel that houses the spirit and soul, providing an earthly covering for our being. It is through our bodies that we express emotions, actions, and desires, and it is through the body that we interact with the physical world.

*Romans 12:4*(NKJV)*– "For as in one body we have many members, and the members do not all have the same function."*

*1 Corinthians 6:19-20*(NKJV)*– "Or do you not know that your body is a temple of the Holy Spirit within you, whom you have from God? You are not your own, for you were bought with a price. So glorify God in your body."*

*2 Corinthians 4:7*(NIV) *– "But we have this treasure in jars of clay, to show that the surpassing power belongs to God and not to us."*

The body is a temple, a sacred dwelling place for the Spirit of God. It must be honoured, cared for, and surrendered to God's will. Though it is temporary and subject to weakness, pain, and ageing, it remains a critical part of our existence and divine assignment on earth.

Understanding the connection between the spirit, soul, and body helps us realise the necessity of divine healing—not just for physical ailments but also for the wounds of the soul and the strengthening of the spirit. Healing must take place holistically, ensuring that every part of our being aligns with God's will, His presence, and His promises.

## 16

# BREAKING FREE

Healing the Wounded Soul

---

The wounds inflicted by trauma, rejection, and painful experiences often go deeper than the physical—they leave scars on the soul that can shape the way we think, feel, and respond to life. Fear, anxiety, bitterness, and emotional numbness can take root, creating strongholds that keep us bound to the pain of the past. However, true healing is possible. This chapter explores the process of breaking free from emotional and psychological strongholds, offering hope and restoration through the power of God's love and divine healing.

When we fall victim to danger, hurt, injury, rejection, or any form of attack, the area that is most affected is our soul. While we may survive a traumatic ordeal physically, the wounds inflicted on our emotions, will, and mind can leave lasting scars. The pain and fear linger long after the event, shaping our responses, thoughts, and sense of security in the world around us.

Perhaps you have endured a robbery, a burglary at your home or business, a carjacking, rape, abuse, a car accident, or molestation. You might have managed to continue with life, yet every time you recall the incident, it feels as though you are reliving the attack, injury, or pain all over again. The trauma does not remain confined to the past—it seeps into your present, affecting your emotions, your thought patterns, and even your behaviour.

In this section, I trust that you will experience God's healing hand of deliverance. I encourage you to allow the Holy Spirit to minister to your heart, to open yourself to His touch, and to receive His healing. If you find yourself constantly battling fear—whether it is the fear of being alone, walking down the street, attending public events, or even going to the shopping mall—or if you struggle with depression and feelings of worthlessness due to past abuse, these are signs that trauma has left a deep imprint on your soul.

The good news is that Jesus Christ is the Healer of broken hearts, the Restorer of shattered souls, and the One who can bring true and lasting healing to every wounded place within you.

## Emotional and Psychological Trauma

When bad things happen, it can take time to overcome the pain and feel safe again. But through God's grace and with the insights that will be shared in this section, I pray that you will experience His healing hand, touching you and making you whole once more.

## What is Emotional and Psychological Trauma?

According to Lawrence Robinson, Melinda Smith, and Jeanne Segal[19], emotional and psychological trauma is the result of extraordinarily stressful events that shatter your sense of security, making you feel helpless in a dangerous world (p.45). This kind of trauma can deeply affect how you function in daily life, often leading to anxiety, depression, fear, and emotional numbness.

There are various causes of emotional and psychological trauma, including:

- **One-time events,** such as an accident, injury, or violent attack—especially if it was unexpected or happened during childhood.

- **Ongoing, relentless stress,** such as living in a crime-ridden neighbourhood, battling a life-threatening illness, or experiencing repeated traumatic events such as bullying, domestic violence, or childhood neglect.

- **Commonly overlooked causes,** such as undergoing surgery (particularly within the first three years of life), experiencing the sudden death of a loved one, suffering the heartbreak of a significant relationship ending, or enduring a deeply humiliating or disappointing event—especially if it involved cruelty from another person.

The aftermath of such trauma can lead to **Post-Traumatic Stress Disorder** (**PTSD**), manifesting through symptoms such as overwhelming fear, insomnia, anxiety, and depression.

For many, the emotional and psychological effects of trauma can be just as debilitating as the event itself. The mind replays the moment over and over again, making it difficult to move forward. The heart struggles with the weight of fear and pain, making it hard to trust, love, or even feel safe in familiar places. The emotions fluctuate between numbness and overwhelming distress, leaving a person feeling lost and helpless.

But despite the weight of trauma, God's promise remains:

**"He heals the brokenhearted and binds up their wounds."** *(Psalm 147:3*[(NKJV)]*)*

This verse is not just poetic—it is a profound revelation of God's healing power. It reassures us that God provides restoration for all three primary components of our being: **spirit, soul, and body**.

The imagery of this scripture paints a clear picture of what medical professionals do when treating physical wounds. A doctor will cleanse the wound and cover it with a clean bandage to promote proper healing. If left exposed, the wound risks infection, and the new cells being formed may dry out, delaying the healing process.

Healing is possible. Restoration is within reach. And freedom from the strongholds of trauma is available through the power of Jesus Christ. His love is the antidote to fear, His presence is the refuge for the wounded, and His peace surpasses all understanding.

The next step is to embark on a journey of healing—one that begins with inviting God into every broken place and allowing Him to restore what has been lost.

Yes, you or a family member might be suffering from **Post-Traumatic Stress Disorder (PTSD)**, which has caused severe anxiety, depression, restlessness, and insomnia due to being a victim of crime, injustice, rape, molestation, an accident, or robbery. The experience may have left lasting emotional wounds, making it incredibly difficult to live a normal, productive life free from fear.

Perhaps your physical injuries have long healed, yet you still struggle to feel a release in your emotions, will, and mind. The pain may have manifested in bitterness, anger, and unforgiveness towards the offender who was responsible for your suffering. You might feel trapped in the cycle of trauma, unable to move forward because the weight of the past is still holding you captive.

**In the same way, God, the Great Physician, does not leave our wounds exposed to further pain or contamination.** He binds them up with His love, mercy, and healing power, ensuring that we recover fully—physically, emotionally, and spiritually. The Lord's care is not superficial; He provides complete healing from the inside out.

**Your season of walking with physical and emotional pain is coming to an end in Jesus's name.**

I know that right now, you might be thinking, **"You don't know what I've been through."** And you are absolutely right—I don't. But **He does.** He sees every tear, every sleepless night, and every anxious thought that has tormented you. He understands your pain in a way no human ever could, and He is offering you an opportunity to receive the deep healing that your soul and body desperately need.

**Don't allow the enemy to convince you that it is not yet time to let go of the pain.** The devil wants to keep you in bondage, but God is calling you into freedom.

The scripture boldly declares:

> **"Behold, now is the accepted time; behold, now is the day of salvation!"** *(2 Corinthians 6:2*[NKJV]*)*

Not tomorrow. **Not next week. Not next year. NOW.**

If you have come this far in this book, I truly believe it is because **God is granting you the grace to let go**—to release the fear, anger, hatred, unforgiveness, bitterness, and resentment that have weighed you down for days, months, or even years.

Your body, soul, and mind were never designed to carry such a heavy burden. **Jesus is ready to lift it off your shoulders.**

Healing and wholeness are yours right now. **Receive it, in Jesus's name.**

# I DECREE AND DECLARE

2 Corinthians 10:5 (NKJV)

*"We demolish arguments and every pretension that sets itself up against the knowledge of God, and we take captive every thought to make it obedient to Christ."*

In **Jesus's mighty name!**

Wherever you are reading this from, I invite you to **prepare your heart** and come **boldly** before God, with **thanksgiving and confidence,** ready to make your requests known to Him. He is near, and His power is available to heal, restore, and deliver.

For the next few moments, I urge you to **speak the Word of God audibly,** to **confess His promises over your life,** and to **pray with faith and expectation.** The power of God is present to **heal, deliver, and set you free.**

Whatever pain, bondage, or struggle you have been carrying—whether it is fear, trauma, affliction, or oppression—**now is the time to release it into the hands of the Lord.**

145

I **truly believe** that as you engage in these prayers and confessions with an open heart, **your life will never be the same again. The chains are breaking, the strongholds are being demolished, and healing is manifesting in Jesus's mighty name!**

## ENTERING DAILY LIVING

You've seen the power of the Word. You've faced the battle and found your footing. Now it's time to live it. Part 3 calls you into a lifestyle of divine protection—not as a momentary shield but as a daily mantle. This final section is about walking in what you've learned, declaring what you believe, and dwelling continually under the banner of Yahweh Nissi.

# PART 3

# LIVING UNDER THE BANNER

This final part brings it all together. Here, faith becomes action and revelation becomes rhythm. You'll read testimonies of protection, learn to make daily prophetic declarations, and begin to cultivate a life that rests in God's unwavering presence. This is not the end of a book—it's the beginning of a lifestyle. Yahweh Nissi isn't just a name you declare. It's the atmosphere you live in.

# 17

# BREAKING FREE

Conquering Fear and Emotional Strongholds

---

Fear, trauma, anger, unforgiveness, and emotional pain have a way of taking root in our hearts, affecting how we think, feel, and live. These strongholds often develop from past experiences—whether through personal loss, crime, betrayal, or injustice—and they can keep us trapped in a cycle of anxiety, bitterness, and unrest. However, God's Word promises freedom, healing, and restoration for every wounded heart. This chapter will guide you through breaking free from these emotional and spiritual strongholds, offering prayers, declarations, and scriptural truths that will empower you to walk in victory and peace.

## Breaking Strongholds of Fear

**Scriptures:** 2 Timothy 1:7[NKJV] *"For God has not given us a spirit of fear, but of power and of love and of a sound mind."*

1 John 4:18[NKJV] *"There is no fear in love; but perfect love casts out fear, because fear involves torment. But he who fears has not been made perfect in love."*

Exodus 14:14 [NIV] *"The Lord will fight for you; you need only to be still."*

Hebrews 13:5b-6 [ESV] *"...for He has said, "I will never leave you nor forsake you." So we can confidently say, "The Lord is my helper; I will not fear; what can man do to me?"*

# Prayer

Heavenly Father, in the name of Jesus Christ, I come boldly before Your throne of grace, with thanksgiving and confidence in my heart, knowing that I will receive Your mercy and grace right now.

I ask for Your forgiveness, Lord, for allowing fear to take root in my life. I acknowledge that through the experiences of crime, robbery, kidnapping, car-jacking, house burglary, abuse, rape, and injustice, fear has entered my heart and mind. But today, I make a divine exchange—I release fear, and I embrace Your perfect love, which casts out all fear.

From this day forward, I refuse to live in fear! I renounce the spirit of fear in every form and every avenue through which it entered my life. Fear, you have no power over me! I cut myself loose from you, in the mighty name of Jesus!

In the name of Jesus Christ, I take authority over the spirit of fear and command you to leave me right now! Leave my mind, my emotions, my will, and my body! I am no longer your dwelling place. I have been redeemed by the blood of Jesus, and I belong to God!

Jesus did not give me a spirit of fear, but of power, love, and a sound mind, therefore, I refuse to accommodate or tolerate any form of fear in my life.

I declare that I am free!
I am free from the control, emotional torment, and manipulation of fear.
I am free from the bondage that has held my will and mind captive.
I am free from the crippling effects of fear that have sought to limit my life.

Thank You, wonderful Jesus, for setting me free! Thank You for restoring peace, confidence, and boldness in my heart. I receive Your perfect love, which overpowers and destroys fear. My mind is sound, my emotions are whole, and my spirit is strong in You!

In the mighty name of Jesus Christ, I am victorious!
Amen!

## Breaking the Stronghold of Insomnia

If you have been battling with insomnia, struggling to find rest at night, declare the Word of God over your life and pray with boldness and faith. Rest is a gift from God, and Scripture specifically mentions that after creating the u(NIV)erse, God rested from His work on the seventh day. The word *Sabbath* literally means to stop, signifying the importance of rest in God's divine design.

Insomnia is an enemy of rest—it is contrary to the will of God. Therefore, do not accept it as a normal part of life. Stand boldly and violently against it in the name of Jesus Christ and receive your miracle today.

**Scripture Declaration:** Psalm 4:8[NIV] *"In peace I will lie down and sleep, for you alone, LORD, make me dwell in safety."*

# Prayer

Heavenly Father, I thank You for Your Word that declares that I will lie down and sleep in peace because You alone make me dwell in safety. I stand on this promise today and receive my divine rest in Jesus' name.

Therefore, in the mighty name of Jesus Christ, I come against every spirit of insomnia that has interfered with my ability to rest as God designed. I bind you, rebuke you, and cast you out in the name of Jesus!

Spirit of insomnia, I command you right now—come out and loose your grip over my peaceful sleep! You are no longer welcome in my life! I renounce you, reject you, and break every hold you have over my rest, my mind, and my body!

Loose your grip and let go of my peace!
Loose your grip and let go of my sleep!
Loose your grip and let go of my mind—right now in the mighty name of Jesus Christ!

I declare and decree that I am free! The chains of restlessness are broken. Every spiritual attack causing sleeplessness is destroyed by the fire of the Holy Spirit. I receive my deliverance and restoration! I will sleep soundly, deeply, and peacefully from this day forward.

Thank You, Lord, for setting me free! Thank You for giving me the sweet sleep that You promised to those who trust in You. My body, mind, and soul are at rest under Your divine protection.

Hallelujah! In the name of Jesus Christ, I receive my miracle and I am victorious!
Amen!

## Breaking Strongholds of Trauma

**Scripture Declaration:** Psalm 34:18[NIV] *"The Lord is close to the broken-hearted and saves those who are crushed in spirit."*

# Prayer

Heavenly Father, I come before You today, deeply grateful for Your healing hand that is touching, restoring, and renewing every area of my soul affected by trauma. Lord, You see the emotional and psychological pain that I have suffered—pain inflicted by both people and the enemy. This trauma has left wounds deep within me, causing distress, fear, and sorrow.

But today, I stand on Your Word! Your promise declares that You are close to the broken-hearted and that You save those who are crushed in spirit. I refuse to accept trauma as my portion, and I reject every form of post-traumatic stress, fear, anxiety, and torment. This is NOT Your will for my life, and I will not walk in bondage any longer.

Father, if at any point I unknowingly accepted trauma as my destiny, I ask for Your forgiveness. I renounce every lie of the enemy that has tried to convince me that I must carry this burden forever! I surrender every scar, every painful memory, and every wound into Your hands.

Holy Spirit, come now and have Your way! Let Your loving and compassionate presence wash over me and remove every remnant of suffering. Touch, restore, and heal every part of my body, soul, and mind that has been affected. I receive complete renewal and divine healing in Jesus' mighty name!

Satan, you have NO authority over me! You came to steal, kill, and destroy, but the Lord Jesus Christ has come that I may have life and life in abundance! You spirit of trauma, depression, severe grief, and hopelessness—I command you right now, in the mighty name of Jesus Christ, COME OUT of my soul and body! Loose your grip and be gone forever! X3

Thank You, Holy Spirit, for Your loving embrace that restores my joy, my peace, and my wholeness. I decree and declare that I am no longer bound by the past! The chains of trauma are broken, my wounds are healed, and my soul is restored!

Hallelujah! I am free in Jesus' mighty name! Amen!

## Breaking Strongholds of Anger

**Scripture Declaration:** Psalm 37:8[NIV] *"Don't give in to worry or anger; it only leads to trouble."*

Ephesians 4:26 [EASY] *"When you are angry, do not do anything bad as a result. Once the day comes to an end, do not continue to be angry."*

# Prayer

Precious Father, I come before You today with humility, acknowledging that I have allowed anger to take hold of my heart. I thank You for Your Word, which instructs us not to give Satan a foothold through unresolved anger. Your scripture clearly warns against letting the sun go down while still harbouring anger.

Lord, I repent for holding onto this anger, especially towards (mention the name of the person or situation). I realise that holding onto resentment has only weighed me down and given the enemy access to my heart and mind. I ask for Your forgiveness right now—cleanse me from every root of bitterness, frustration, and rage that has settled in my soul.

Father, I release and forgive the one who has hurt me. Grant me the grace and strength to fully let go of this anger, so that it no longer has power over me. I refuse to allow past offences to dictate my emotions, my reactions, or my future.

In the name of Jesus Christ, I renounce every spirit that has entered through the door of anger. I break every chain that has bound me to frustration, rage, resentment, and hostility. In Jesus' mighty name, I cut myself loose from every spirit of anger!

Right now, in the mighty name of Jesus Christ, I command every spirit of anger to come out of my soul and body! Leave my life NOW! You are no longer welcome! X3

I declare that I am free from the power of anger! I receive the peace of Christ that surpasses all understanding. His love fills my heart, His peace floods my soul, and His joy strengthens my spirit.

Thank You, Lord, for Your mighty hand of healing and deliverance. I walk in freedom, peace, and divine restoration, in Jesus' mighty name!

Hallelujah! Amen!

## Breaking Strongholds of Hatred

**Scripture Declaration:** 1 John 2:9-11[NIV] *"Anyone who claims to be in the light but hates a brother or sister is still in the darkness. Anyone who loves their brother and sister lives in the light, and there is nothing in them to make them stumble. But anyone who hates a brother or sister is in the darkness and walks around in the darkness. They do not know where they are going, because the darkness has blinded them."*

Proverbs 10:12[NIV] *"Hatred stirs up conflict, but love covers over all wrongs."*

# Prayer

Lord Jesus, I come before You with a heart of repentance, acknowledging that I have allowed hatred to take root in my heart because of the pain, betrayal, and injustice I have suffered. Your Word is truth, and today, I submit to that truth. Your Word says that if I hold hatred in my heart, I am walking in darkness. Lord, I no longer want to live in darkness!

I ask for Your forgiveness, Father. I repent for allowing hatred to control my thoughts, my emotions, and my actions. I acknowledge that the pain I have endured—whether through crime, abuse, injustice, rejection, betrayal, or loss—has left wounds in my heart. But today, I choose freedom over bondage, and love over hatred.

159

In the mighty name of Jesus Christ, I renounce every spirit of hatred, resentment, and bitterness that has taken hold of my heart. I declare that hatred has no place in me! I release all hatred towards (mention the names or situation), and I surrender it to You, Lord.

Every spirit of hatred, I command you in the name of Jesus Christ—come out! Leave my will, my mind, my emotions, and my body! X3

You are no longer welcome! I evict you by the power of the blood of Jesus!

I declare that I am free from the spirit of hatred! I receive the love of God into my heart, and I choose to walk in His light. I refuse to be held captive by darkness any longer. Lord, thank You for breaking the chains of hatred in my life and setting me free.

I receive Your love, peace, and restoration right now, in Jesus' mighty name!

Hallelujah! Amen!

## Breaking Strongholds of Unforgiveness

**Scripture Declaration:** Mark 11:25[(NKJV)] *"And whenever you stand praying, forgive, if you have anything against anyone, so that your Father also who is in heaven may forgive you your trespasses."*

Matthew 18:21-22[(NKJV)] *"Then Peter came up and said to him, 'Lord, how often will my brother sin against me, and I forgive him? As many as seven times?' Jesus said to him, 'I do not say to you seven times, but seventy-seven times.'"*

Matthew 6:14-15[(NKJV)] *"For if you forgive others their trespasses, your heavenly Father will also forgive you, but if you do not forgive others their trespasses, neither will your Father forgive your trespasses."*

# Prayer

Oh Lord, I humbly come before Your throne of grace today, seeking Your mercy and forgiveness. I acknowledge that because of the deep pain, disappointment, and suffering I have endured, I allowed myself to justify harbouring unforgiveness in my heart. I believed that my wounds and grievances gave me the right to hold onto bitterness. But today, Lord, I surrender it all to You.

Your Word teaches me that forgiveness is not optional, and if I desire to be forgiven, I must extend that same grace to others. I cannot receive what I refuse to give. Therefore, Lord, I choose to release every person who has wronged, betrayed, or hurt me. I refuse to allow unforgiveness to poison my soul any longer.

In the mighty name of Jesus Christ, I renounce every spirit of unforgiveness! I cut myself loose from every root of bitterness, resentment, and emotional pain that has weighed me down for so long. Unforgiveness has no place in my life!

Every spirit of unforgiveness, I command you in Jesus' mighty name—come out of my heart! X3

You have been holding me back, preventing me from experiencing the fullness of God's love and peace. I reject you, and I refuse to give you any more control over my life!

Lord, I thank You for touching and healing my heart today. I receive Your peace, joy, and freedom right now! I declare that I am a new person, free from unforgiveness, bitterness, anger, and resentment. Thank You, Jesus, for setting me free!

Hallelujah! I walk in the light of forgiveness, in the mighty name of Jesus Christ! Amen.

---

I honour the powerful step of faith you have taken today! By allowing the Holy Spirit to minister healing and deliverance to you, you have positioned yourself to walk in a new dimension of grace with a renewed mind and a heart free from bondage. Every lie of the enemy that once held you captive—whether through thoughts, words, or experiences—has now been replaced by the truth of God's Word and the power of prayer. What a victorious combination to living an overcoming life in Jesus Christ!

## The Word of God declares:

*"Do not conform to the pattern of this world, but be transformed by the renewing of your mind. Then you will be able to test and approve what God's will is—his good, pleasing and perfect will."* — Romans 12:2[NKJV]

As you continue on this journey, may God's truth anchor your heart, His peace guard your mind, and His presence fill every area of your life. You are free, healed, and set apart for His divine purpose! Hallelujah!

# 18

# BREAKING FREE

Testimonies of Divine Protection and Miracles

Throughout our lives, there are moments when we encounter situations that defy logic—moments where we should have faced harm, loss, or destruction, yet something supernatural intervened. In this chapter, you will read testimonies of God's divine protection, safety, and miraculous deliverance. These real-life accounts serve as undeniable evidence that God is present, active, and deeply involved in the lives of His people. Whether through a life-altering accident, an unexpected escape from danger, or a transformation that seemed impossible, these testimonies will remind you of the power of faith, prayer, and the unfailing hand of God at work.

In this chapter, I will share a few testimonies—both my own and those of others—of experiencing God's divine safety, protection, comfort, and guidance in various situations. These accounts stand as undeniable proof that God's protection is real, His presence is near, and His faithfulness is unwavering.

One particular testimony that remains vivid in my memory is an experience I had in April 2010, on a rainy day in Johannesburg. I was on my way home from work, navigating through the busy intersection in Bruma along the R24. As I sat in my car waiting for the traffic light to change, something in my rear-view mirror caught my attention.

A car was approaching rapidly from behind, seemingly out of control. In a split second, before I could fully comprehend what was happening, I heard a loud crash—a sudden impact from behind pushed my car forcefully into the middle of the intersection, directly into the path of fast-moving vehicles.

Time seemed to slow down. As my car lurched forward, I braced myself, expecting the worst. I could hear the blaring of horns and saw vehicles moving swiftly on both sides. But in that critical moment, something miraculous happened. Not a single passing car hit me. By the grace of God, my car came to a complete stop unscathed, despite being thrust into the danger zone.

I was shaking from the shock, my mind racing with disbelief at what had just transpired. My first thought was that my car must be severely damaged, considering the force of the impact. Being a hatchback, I assumed the rear of my vehicle would be completely crushed.

When I finally gathered the courage to step out and assess the damage, what I saw astonished me. My car had only a minor scratch on the bumper and boot—nothing compared to the devastation I had imagined. But when I looked at the other driver's car, it was a complete wreck. The front of his vehicle was destroyed, his airbags had deployed, and the damage was extensive.

At that moment, I realised I had witnessed the tangible hand of God's protection. It was a weapon formed against me, but it could not prosper, because Yahweh Nissi—the Lord my Banner—was with me. Hallelujah! Praise God for His wonders among men!

I thank God that I am alive today to testify of His goodness. Perhaps you or someone in your family has had a similar experience—a moment where God's protection became evident and turned into a powerful testimony.

These miracles, signs, and wonders are divine markers, pointing us to Jesus, drawing us to repentance, and reminding us that God is with us. Whenever we witness His mighty hand in our lives, it strengthens our faith, making it relentless and unshakable.

*"He came to Jesus at night and said, 'Rabbi, we know that you are a teacher who has come from God. For no one could perform the signs you are doing if God were not with him.'"* — John 3:2[NKJV]

There are several scriptures in the Bible that encourage us to share what God has done, as a reminder to ourselves, to others, and to future generations. When we testify, we proclaim His goodness, mercy, and lovingkindness, demonstrating a heart of gratitude and exalting His name. Our testimonies serve as a witness of His power, strengthening the faith of others and glorifying Him before all people.

## The Word of God declares:

"My mouth will tell of your righteous acts, of your deeds of salvation all the day,
for their number is past my knowledge. With the mighty deeds of the Lord God I will come;
I will remind them of your righteousness, yours alone."
— *Psalm 71:15-16*[ESV]

"Come and hear, all you who fear God, and I will tell what he has done for my soul." — *Psalm 66:16*

"One generation shall commend your works to another, and shall declare your mighty acts." — *Psalm 145:4* [ESV]

"Declare his glory among the nations, his marvellous works among all the peoples!" — *Psalm 96:3* [ESV]

"And they overcame him because of the blood of the Lamb and because of the word of their testimony, and they did not love their life even when faced with death." — *Revelation 12:11* [ESV]

These scriptures affirm the power of testimony—it is not just a personal experience, but a spiritual weapon. When we declare what the Lord has done, we remind ourselves and others of His faithfulness, reinforcing the truth that He is the same yesterday, today, and forever.

May our lives be a living testimony of His greatness, and may we always be bold in proclaiming the mighty works of the Lord!

May these testimonies serve as a reminder that God is ever-present, watching over His children, shielding them from harm, and proving time and again that He is our refuge, fortress, and deliverer. Amen!

---

TESTIMONY 1

# FROM CHAINS TO FREEDOM: THE TESTIMONY OF CLINTON STEWARD

### My Impactful Testimony of God's Divine Safety and Protection

*"When I first met my spiritual father, Pastor Realton Suliman, in 2017, I was immediately struck by his deep love for God. At the time, my life was completely broken—I was caught up in drugs, alcohol abuse, and criminal activities. But God, in His mercy, had already set a divine appointment for me.*

*I remember the day so vividly. Pastor Realton was out in the streets of Ennerdale, Extension 6, passionately preaching the gospel of Jesus Christ during an outreach mission. I was sitting in my garage when I overheard his powerful testimony about how God had saved him and transformed his life. His words gripped my heart in a way I had never experienced before.*

*As he preached, something inside me stirred. Towards the end of the sermon, he made an altar call, asking if anyone wanted to accept Jesus as their Lord and Saviour. I don't even know how, but something stronger than my doubts and fears pushed me forward. I stepped out for prayer, and right there on the street, I was set free!*

*That moment changed everything for me. I was instantly delivered—from drug addiction, alcohol abuse, and a life of crime. The chains that had held me captive for years broke in an instant. My life has never been the same since!*

*From that day on, my journey with Pastor Realton became one of the greatest experiences of my life. I remember one particular night during a healing and deliverance service. As Pastor Realton was preaching, the power of God began to move mightily in the tent. People started manifesting, demons were being cast out, and the presence of God was tangible. It was something I had never seen before! At first, many of us were shocked and even scared. We had never witnessed God using someone so powerfully to set people free. Some of us even looked for the nearest exit to run out of the tent!*

*But something deeper was happening inside me. I was witnessing God's power at work in ways I had never imagined. After that night, going to church became like running a marathon—we could not wait to get to the next service! We were hungry for more of God, eager to see His power change lives.*

Today, I praise God for this miraculous testimony of salvation, deliverance, and divine protection. Jesus completely turned my life around.

Hallelujah! Praise God for His wonders among us! What an incredible testimony of transformation, restoration, and divine protection!

---

TESTIMONY 2

# SUPERNATURAL PROTECTION IN A CAR ACCIDENT – THE TESTIMONY OF MERCIA MURISON

"In April 2020, I experienced God's supernatural hand of protection in a vehicle accident that could have taken my life. It was the beginning of a new week, just after the Easter weekend, and as usual, I had to make my early morning commute from Ennerdale to Benoni for work. To ensure that I arrived on time, I had to leave before 5 am each morning.

However, on that fateful morning, something felt different. The atmosphere was heavier than usual, and it was darker outside due to the cloudy skies and persistent rain. As I woke up, I had an overwhelming feeling not to go to work, but being a new employee on probation, I felt pressured to push through.

*I struggled internally, walking around the house, debating whether to trust my instinct and stay home or gather enough courage to go. Weeks before this, I had a dream in which I saw myself rolling, but hands were cushioning me. In the dream, I felt no pain or fear, but at the time, I dismissed it as meaningless. Only after the accident did I realise that the Holy Spirit had been warning me all along.*

*Despite all these internal warnings, I still ignored them and got into my car. As part of my usual morning routine, I switched on my radio to play gospel music and plugged my phone into the charger. Unexpectedly, the radio and charger fuse blew, leaving me in silence. This startled me, but I was too focused on getting to work on time to reflect on the significance of this. Instead, I began to pray in tongues, following what I had been taught by my pastor, Pastor Realton Suliman.*

*As I continued praying and quoting scriptures, I went to pick up my passenger. She was unusually delayed, taking longer than expected to come out of her house. When she finally got into the car, I noticed that she had overslept—her hair was uncombed, and she wasn't neatly dressed. She yawned uncontrollably, telling me that her family had just returned from a long weekend trip.*

*Even as these signs continued to confirm the strong feeling I had earlier, I still ignored them. My only concern was reaching work on time and avoiding any trouble with my employer.*

*As we got onto the N1 freeway, the rain continued falling, making visibility and road conditions even worse. At that moment, a very impatient driver appeared behind me, aggressively flashing his brights, pressuring me to move out of the way. I panicked and started accelerating to switch lanes.*

*As I crossed over to the other side, I suddenly felt like I was driving on a bed of water. The car lost all traction, and before I knew it, we were spinning out of control. The vehicle swerved violently from left to right, and then, in an instant, we were thrown off the road.*

*At that moment, everything felt surreal. The car began rolling over multiple times, eventually landing upside down on my side. The world around me became eerily quiet, and all I could smell was soil.*

*Despite the impact, my mind remained alert, and my first instinct was to get out of the vehicle. I had a full tank of fuel, the ignition was still on, and the car was overturned, creating an extremely dangerous situation. My passenger was struggling to undo her seatbelt, while I frantically tried every door and window to find an escape.*

*Then something miraculous happened.*

*I found a window that was completely missing, but what struck me was that there was no shattered glass anywhere. It was as if someone had carefully removed the entire window, creating a perfect way for us to escape.*

*We crawled out of the opening, and help arrived soon after.*

*Amazingly, I walked away without a single scratch, only minor whiplash. My passenger suffered only a fractured finger. Given the severity of the accident, this was nothing short of God's divine intervention.*

*Pastor Realton had taught me how to pray and use scripture to activate the power of God in my life. Through this experience, I witnessed first-hand that God was present every step of the way. Looking back, I now see that He had been trying to warn me all along, through the uneasy feeling in my spirit, through the dream, and even through the delayed morning events. Yet, even though I ignored the warnings, He still protected me.*

*Before joining Eagle Family Church, I struggled to have a relationship with God. I lacked understanding and didn't truly know how to hear His voice. But through my spiritual journey and under the guidance of my pastor, I learned how to walk closely with God. This accident solidified my faith and confirmed that God is real, that He speaks to His children, and that He is always present, guiding, protecting, and preserving us."*

Hallelujah! What a powerful testimony of God's faithfulness, divine protection, and supernatural guidance!

# 19

# THE PRESENCE OF GOD

Our Ultimate Refuge and Protection

---

The presence of God is not just a concept—it is a living reality that guarantees divine protection, guidance, and peace. Throughout Scripture, His presence has been demonstrated through the Ark of the Covenant, the manifestation of His glory, and now, through the indwelling Holy Spirit.

This chapter explores how God's presence has always been the ultimate shield for His people, ensuring supernatural deliverance, provision, and security. As believers, we are no longer reliant on symbols of His presence but have direct access to Him through the Holy Spirit. In Him, we find refuge, strength, and the assurance that no harm can prevail against us.

May this chapter awaken in you a deeper awareness of God's presence, drawing you into greater faith and confidence in His unfailing protection.

It is impossible to discuss God's divine protection without acknowledging the significance of His presence. Throughout the Old Testament, two major themes stand out: the glory of the Lord and the Ark of the Covenant—both of which symbolise God's presence, power, and protection.

Many religious traditions hold the conviction that God's presence brings supernatural security and shielding from harm. This belief is deeply rooted in Scripture, which repeatedly provides evidence of God's omnipotence in protecting His people. The following biblical accounts illustrate this profound truth of divine protection.

## The Ark of the Covenant: A Symbol of God's Presence and Protection

The Ark of the Covenant was a sacred chest, constructed by the Israelites under God's explicit instructions. It served as a tangible representation of God's dwelling among His people—offering guidance, protection, and direction.

Exodus 25:10–22[(NKJV)] records God's instruction to Moses regarding the Ark's construction:

*"Have them make an ark of acacia wood... I will meet with you there and give you all of my instructions for the Israelites, above*

*the cover between the two cherubim that are over the ark of the covenant law."*

This passage highlights that the Ark was not merely an object of religious reverence but a place of divine encounter where God would speak with Moses.

## The Ark and Divine Protection

In Joshua 3:14–17[(NKJV)], the Ark played a pivotal role in securing safe passage for the Israelites across the Jordan River:

*"The priests bearing the ark of the covenant preceded the people when they broke camp to cross the Jordan... Israel continued to cross the Jordan until they had all reached dry land, and at that point, the priests bearing the ark of the Lord's covenant halted and stood on dry land in the middle of the river."*

This miraculous event reinforces the reality that God's presence guarantees divine protection and provision. As long as the Ark was with them, the Israelites experienced miraculous victories, guidance, and security.

## A Misplaced Reliance on Symbols Over God's Presence

In 1 Samuel 4:3-5[(NIV)], the Israelites suffered defeat at the hands of the Philistines, prompting them to bring the Ark of the Covenant into battle, believing it would secure their victory:

*"Why did the Lord bring defeat on us today before the Philistines?" the elders of Israel questioned. "Let us carry the ark*

*of the Lord's covenant from Shiloh, so that He can accompany us and deliver us from the hands of our adversaries. "*

However, their reliance on the Ark as a mere object—instead of on God Himself—did not lead to victory. The Israelites were defeated, and the Ark was captured by the Philistines.

This passage serves as a powerful reminder that true protection is not found in religious symbols but in an intimate, obedient relationship with God. Faith and reliance on God's presence— rather than merely external symbols—are what truly bring divine protection and favour.

## The Presence of God: A Shield for His People

From these scriptures, we see that God's presence is our ultimate refuge. The Ark of the Covenant, though significant, was only a representation of what we now have through Christ Jesus—direct access to God's divine presence and protection.

Psalm 91:1-2[NIV] assures us:
*"Whoever dwells in the shelter of the Most High will rest in the shadow of the Almighty. I will say of the Lord, 'He is my refuge and my fortress, my God, in whom I trust.'"*

As believers today, we no longer rely on physical representations like the Ark but on the indwelling presence of God through the Holy Spirit. His presence is our ultimate place of safety, and in Him, we find supernatural protection, deliverance, and peace.

Hallelujah! What a mighty and faithful God we serve!

## The Glory of the Lord

The glory of the Lord is a profound manifestation of God's presence, power, and majesty. Throughout Scripture, the glory of God is often symbolised by a cloud, fire, or radiant light, signifying His divine presence and protection.

## God's Glory as a Guiding and Protecting Presence

In Exodus 40:34–38[(NKJV)], we see a remarkable display of God's glory descending upon the Tabernacle:

> "*Then the cloud covered the Tabernacle, and the Lord's splendour filled it. Throughout their whole journey, the Israelites would depart anytime the cloud lifted from over the Tabernacle; however, if it did not, they would wait until the cloud lifted before setting away.*"

This passage illustrates how God's glory led, protected, and directed the Israelites as they journeyed through the wilderness. His presence was not merely symbolic but a tangible reality—offering supernatural guidance, provision, and security.

The Israelites did not move unless the cloud lifted—a clear sign that God's presence determined their course. This is a powerful demonstration of how those who trust in God and follow His presence will always be divinely led and protected.

## The Glory of God Filling the Temple

A similar manifestation of God's glory is recorded in 2 Chronicles 7:1-3[(NKJV)], when Solomon dedicated the Temple to the Lord:

*"The splendour of the Lord filled the temple, and when Solomon had finished praying, fire descended from heaven and devoured the burnt offering and the sacrifices. With their faces on the ground, the Israelites knelt on the pavement and worshipped and gave thanks to the Lord as they witnessed the fire falling and the glory of the Lord above the temple."*

This passage reveals God's overwhelming presence descending upon His holy place, signifying His approval and acceptance of the Temple as a dwelling place for His name.

The fire from heaven was a sign of divine intervention, consuming the sacrifice and marking God's favour and authority. The people, witnessing such a powerful event, fell on their faces in awe and worshipped God, acknowledging His majesty and holiness.

## The Glory of God as Our Protection

The glory of the Lord is not only a sign of His majesty but also a shield of divine protection. Just as the Israelites were led by the cloud, we, as believers, are guided by the Holy Spirit—our ever-present help, comfort, and defence.

Isaiah 4:5[(NIV)] assures us:
*"Then the Lord will create over all of Mount Zion and over*

*those who assemble there a cloud of smoke by day and a glow of flaming fire by night; over everything the glory will be a canopy."*

This prophecy speaks of God's protective covering over His people—His glory acting as a supernatural shield against harm, fear, and danger.

The glory of God is not just a past reality but a present and living force. Through Jesus Christ, we now have direct access to His glory, experiencing His presence, protection, and power daily. His glory is our refuge, our guide, and our source of victory!

## The Connection to the Holy Spirit

The Holy Spirit is the manifest presence of God dwelling among His people, offering divine protection, comfort, and guidance. In the New Testament, we see how God's presence continues through the Holy Spirit, empowering believers to walk in authority, peace, and supernatural safety.

## The Holy Spirit as Our Advocate and Helper

In John 14:16–17[(NKJV)], Jesus reassures His disciples of the coming of the Holy Spirit:

*"And I will ask the Father, and He will give you another Advocate—the Spirit of truth—to aid you and be with you forever. Because it does not see Him and does not know Him, the world cannot accept Him. You are aware of Him, though, as He coexists and will always be a part of you."*

Here, Jesus introduces the Holy Spirit as the Advocate (Helper, Comforter, and Guide). The word "another" in Greek is "*allos*"[20], meaning *another of the same kind*—signifying that the Holy Spirit would carry on the same work of Jesus, ensuring that God's presence would never leave His people.

This promise means that believers are never alone. The Holy Spirit dwells within us, offering guidance, protection, and supernatural peace in all circumstances.

## The Holy Spirit Empowers Believers

The arrival of the Holy Spirit on the Day of Pentecost further proves that God's presence is now within His people, actively equipping them for spiritual battles, divine protection, and supernatural works.

In Acts 2:1–4[(NIV)], we see this extraordinary event:

> "*They were all together in one location on the day of Pentecost. They were seated there when all of a sudden there was a sound throughout the entire house that sounded like a strong wind coming from above. As the Holy Spirit empowered them, they were all filled with Him and started speaking in tongues.*"

This moment of divine empowerment signifies that God's presence is no longer confined to the Ark of the Covenant or the Temple—but now resides within His people through the Holy Spirit.

The power of the Holy Spirit is the believer's source of supernatural strength, discernment, and spiritual authority. When we are filled with His presence, we experience:

- Boldness to overcome fear and intimidation

- Protection from spiritual and physical harm

- Supernatural peace in times of distress

- The ability to walk in wisdom and discernment

## The Holy Spirit as Our Divine Protector

The Scriptures reveal that God's presence—whether through the Ark of the Covenant, His glory, or the Holy Spirit—creates a powerful shield around His people.

Isaiah 59:19[(NKJV)] declares:
*"When the enemy shall come in like a flood, the Spirit of the Lord shall lift up a standard against him."*

This means that the Holy Spirit actively defends us from the enemy's attacks, standing as a barrier against harm, deception, and destruction.

## God's Presence Brings Divine Peace and Comfort

Through the Holy Spirit, God's presence offers divine peace in the midst of trials and storms. Jesus Himself affirmed this in John 14:27[(NKJV)]:

*"Peace I leave with you; my peace I give you. I do not give to you as the world gives. Do not let your hearts be troubled and do not be afraid."*

The presence of the Holy Spirit in our lives is God's divine assurance that we are not alone, not vulnerable, and not without protection. His peace surpasses all human understanding, guarding our hearts and minds in the midst of danger, uncertainty, and trials.

## Walking in the Power and Protection of the Holy Spirit

Believers are called to walk in the fullness of the Holy Spirit— allowing His wisdom, strength, and supernatural presence to guide them daily. When we yield to the Spirit, we operate under divine protection, discernment, and victory.

The Holy Spirit is our eternal Comforter, our divine Protector, and our ever-present Guide. As we remain sensitive to His leading, we will always find ourselves in the safety of God's perfect will.

Hallelujah! The presence of the Lord is our greatest refuge!

# 20

# DIVINE PROTECTIONS

Understanding God's Covenant of Safety

---

Throughout history, in His infinite wisdom, grace, and mercy, God has continually provided divine safety and protection for humanity. This protection has been demonstrated in various ways and across different periods. Under the Old Covenant, the Israelites were required to follow strict laws and rituals to obtain God's protection. One such example was the application of the blood of a lamb during the Passover to ensure their safety from divine judgment. Additionally, they were expected to live in obedience to God's commandments, as their protection and blessings were conditional upon their faithfulness. In this chapter, we will explore the biblical foundations of divine protection, how it operated under law, but now operates under grace, and what it means for believers today. Discover how faith in Jesus Christ grants not only eternal salvation but also supernatural preservation in the present.

The following scriptures illustrate these principles:

### Exodus 12:13(NKJV)

*"The blood on the doorposts will be a sign to mark the houses in which you live. When I see the blood, I will pass over you and will not harm you when I punish the Egyptians."*

### Deuteronomy 28:1-14(NKJV)

*"And if you faithfully obey the voice of the LORD your God, being careful to do all his commandments that I command you today, the LORD your God will set you high above all the nations of the earth. And all these blessings shall come upon you and overtake you, if you obey the voice of the LORD your God."*

The passage continues to detail the many blessings that would follow obedience, including victory over enemies, prosperity, fruitfulness, and divine protection. However, under this covenant, divine protection was heavily reliant on works—individuals had to earn God's favour through strict adherence to the Law.

## The New Covenant—The Burden Carried by Christ

Under the New Covenant, the burden of divine protection, provision, healing, grace, mercy, and favour has been placed entirely on Jesus Christ. Through His sacrificial death and resurrection, divine protection is now freely available to all who believe in Him and surrender their lives to His lordship.

## John 1:17<sup>(NKJV)</sup>

*"For the law was given through Moses; grace and truth came through Jesus Christ."*

## James 2:10<sup>(NKJV)</sup>

*"For whoever keeps the whole law and yet stumbles at just one point is guilty of breaking all of it."*

The Old Covenant placed impossible demands on humanity due to the fallen nature of man. It was impossible to uphold the law perfectly, and even a single failure made one guilty of breaking the entire law. However, Christ fulfilled the righteous requirements of the Law on our behalf, making way for grace, protection, and salvation through faith alone.

## Romans 8:3-4<sup>(NKJV)</sup>

*"For what the law was powerless to do because it was weakened by the flesh, God did by sending His own Son in the likeness of sinful flesh to be a sin offering. And so He condemned sin in the flesh, in order that the righteous requirement of the law might be fully met in us, who do not live according to the flesh but according to the Spirit."*

## 2 Corinthians 5:21<sup>(NKJV)</sup>

*"For He made Him who knew no sin to be sin for us, that we might become the righteousness of God in Him."*

## Ephesians 2:8<sup>(NKJV)</sup>

*"For it is by grace you have been saved, through faith—and this is not from yourselves, it is the gift of God."*

## John 14:6<sup>(NKJV)</sup>

*"Jesus answered, 'I am the way and the truth and the life. No one comes to the Father except through me.'"*

Jesus became the ultimate, unblemished sacrificial Lamb for all humanity. Through Him, we now have forgiveness, justification, righteousness, eternal life, mercy, grace, peace, healing, and divine protection. He is not just the way to the Father—He is also the way to supernatural safety and preservation.

## Physical Protection Under the New Covenant

Some argue that divine protection in the New Covenant only refers to the salvation of our souls for eternity, rather than physical safety and deliverance from danger. However, this view does not align with scripture. The Bible provides numerous accounts of God's physical protection and preservation of His people.

For example, Paul and Silas endured severe persecution and beatings, yet their lives were preserved so they could continue spreading the Gospel:

## Acts 16:25-31<sup>(NKJV)</sup>

*"About midnight Paul and Silas were praying and singing hymns to God, and the prisoners were listening to them. Suddenly, there was a great earthquake, so that the foundations of the prison were shaken. Immediately, all the doors were opened, and*

*everyone's chains were unfastened. When the jailer woke and saw that the prison doors were open, he drew his sword and was about to kill himself, supposing that the prisoners had escaped. But Paul cried with a loud voice, 'Do not harm yourself, for we are all here.' The jailer called for lights, rushed in, and, trembling with fear, fell down before Paul and Silas. Then he brought them out and asked, 'Sirs, what must I do to be saved?' They replied, 'Believe in the Lord Jesus, and you will be saved—you and your household.'"*

This powerful testimony shows that divine protection is not just a spiritual concept—God actively intervenes in physical circumstances to fulfill His greater purpose.

## Divine Protection as a Sign of God's Presence

The earthquake that freed Paul and Silas was not just a random event—it was a supernatural sign of God's intervention. The jailer witnessed the power of God and, as a result, asked one of the most important questions in history:

"What must I do to be saved?"

Paul and Silas answered with the life-changing truth:

"Believe in the Lord Jesus, and you will be saved—you and your household."

This event confirms that God's protection often serves as a powerful testimony to draw people to salvation in Jesus Christ.

## God's Protection Is a Gift to Those Who Believe

Throughout scripture, we see repeated demonstrations of God's protection—not just for eternity, but also in the here and now. Jesus Christ fulfilled the requirements of the Law, making divine protection available to all who believe in Him.

We are no longer required to earn divine protection through rituals or works, but we are called to walk in faith, believing that Christ's finished work has secured our safety.

If you have never trusted in Jesus Christ for your salvation and protection, today is the perfect time to surrender your life to Him. The promise of divine safety is not just for eternity—it is for every area of your life.

Just as the jailer asked Paul and Silas, the same question is being asked today:

"What must I do to be saved?"

The answer remains unchanged:

"Believe in the Lord Jesus, and you will be saved—you and your household." *(Acts 16:31*[NKJV]*)*

Divine safety, protection, and eternal security are freely given through Christ alone. Will you receive them today?

## 21

# WALKING IN DIVINE PROTECTION

Keys to Living Under God's Covering

---

God's protection is not a mystery—it is a promise available to all who align themselves with His Word, His presence, and His principles. In this chapter, we will explore the biblical keys to experiencing divine safety and security. From faith in Christ to walking in love, trusting God, and living a surrendered life, these foundational truths will empower you to dwell under His covering. Discover how to move from fear to faith, from uncertainty to confidence, and from vulnerability to supernatural protection in Him.

The Bible provides clear guidance on how to obtain and walk in God's divine protection. These principles, grounded in Scripture, help us align ourselves with His will so that we may experience His covering in every area of life.

## Believe in the Lord Jesus Christ

The foundation of divine protection is found in faith in Jesus Christ. The Apostle Paul makes this declaration in:

*"And they said, 'Believe in the Lord Jesus, and you will be saved, you and your household.'"* Acts 16:31[(NKJV)]

The Greek verb *"sozo"*—translated as *saved* in this verse—encompasses more than just salvation. It speaks of wholeness, restoration, healing, deliverance, and preservation. This verse provides a complete picture of what happens when we believe in Jesus and accept Him into our lives.

## Trust in God Completely

Belief in Christ is not just a mental acknowledgment but an active trust in His wisdom and power. This trust is essential to experiencing His divine protection.

*"Trust in the Lord with all your heart and lean not on your own understanding; in all your ways submit to him, and he will make your paths straight."* Proverbs 3:5-6[(NIV)]

To trust in God means to rely on His wisdom and guidance rather than depending on our own limited understanding. When we acknowledge Him in every decision, He ensures that our paths are made straight, free from unnecessary harm and danger.

191

## Confess with Your Mouth

Faith is not only believed in the heart—it must also be confessed with the mouth. The spoken word carries power, and our confession aligns us with God's promises.

*"For it is with your heart that you believe and are justified, and it is with your mouth that you profess your faith and are saved."*
Romans 10:10[NKJV]

Our declaration of faith not only confirms our salvation but also invokes divine protection. When we speak God's Word, we reinforce His truth in our lives and resist the enemy's plans against us.

## Walk in Love

Another key principle to experiencing God's divine safety is walking in love. Love is a defining characteristic of those who belong to Christ, and it protects and guides us in ways we may not always realise.

*"By this everyone will know that you are my disciples, if you love one another."* John 13:35[NKJV]

True discipleship is demonstrated through love—not just in words, but in actions. When we walk in love, we walk in obedience to God, and obedience brings His covering and protection.

## The Power of Love in Protection

The Apostle Paul provides a profound description of love and its role in our spiritual walk:

*"If I speak in the tongues of men or of angels, but do not have love, I am only a resounding gong or a clanging cymbal. If I have the gift of prophecy and can fathom all mysteries and all knowledge, and if I have a faith that can move mountains, but do not have love, I am nothing. If I give all I possess to the poor and give over my body to hardship that I may boast, but do not have love, I gain nothing.*

*"Love is patient, love is kind. It does not envy, it does not boast, it is not proud. It does not dishonour others, it is not self-seeking, it is not easily angered, it keeps no record of wrongs. Love does not delight in evil but rejoices with the truth. It always protects, always trusts, always hopes, always perseveres. Love never fails."*
1 Corinthians 13:1-8[(NKJV)]

This passage reveals that love is not just a feeling but an active force. Love is patient, kind, selfless, and enduring—it does not dwell on wrongs or hold grudges. Walking in love ensures that we remain under the covering of God's protection.

It is important to recognise that love is not a weakness, but rather a supernatural force that shields us from harm. Scripture even states:

*"Love always protects."*

193

When we love others, we not only reflect Christ, but we also position ourselves within His divine safety.

## Living in God's Protection

Experiencing God's divine protection requires:

- Believing in Jesus Christ as Lord and Saviour

- Trusting in Him completely instead of relying on our own understanding

- Confessing His promises over our lives

- Walking in love—towards God and others

By following these biblical principles, we position ourselves under God's covering, ensuring that His divine safety and provision follow us all the days of our lives.

## Live for Him

Walking in divine protection requires not only faith but also a life surrendered to God. Jesus made it clear that following Him requires denying ourselves, committing fully, and walking in obedience.

*"Then he said to them all: 'Whoever wants to be my disciple must deny themselves and take up their cross daily and follow me.'"* Luke 9:23(NKJV)

This verse highlights the daily commitment required to walk as a true disciple of Christ. To experience the fullness of His divine safety and protection, we must live for Him, placing our trust in His guidance and surrendering our will to His.

*"But when the Helper comes, whom I shall send to you from the Father, the Spirit of truth who proceeds from the Father, He will testify of Me."* John 15:26[(NKJV)]

God did not leave us to walk this journey alone. Through Jesus Christ, grace and truth came, and He provided the Holy Spirit as our Helper—enabling us to live a life of faith, holiness, and righteousness.

While we are under a new and better covenant, we are still expected to live in a way that honours God, reflecting His holiness in our thoughts, actions, and daily walk.

*"What shall we say, then? Shall we go on sinning so that grace may increase? By no means! We are those who have died to sin; how can we live in it any longer?"* Romans 6:1-2[(NKJV)]

Grace is not a license to sin—rather, it empowers us to live righteously, knowing that our old sinful nature was crucified with Christ.

*"No one who is born of God will continue to sin, because God's seed remains in them; they cannot go on sinning, because they have been born of God."* 1 John 3:9[(NIV)]

To truly walk under God's protection, we must embrace the new nature given to us through Christ. We no longer live by our own strength but through faith in Him.

## Faith: The Key to Divine Safety and Protection

To walk in the reality of Yahweh Nissi, the Lord our Banner, our Refuge, and our Defender, we must develop a strong life of faith. This means depending not on our own natural abilities, but on the supremacy of God.

> *"Now the just shall live by faith."* Hebrews 10:38[NKJV]

It is faith that enables us to persevere in times of persecution, to overcome spiritual and natural threats, and to remain steadfast in the face of adversity.

When confronted with danger, challenges, and trials, our faith must remain unshaken. It is through faith that we will continue to pray, confess the Word, and stand firm in God's promises.

- It is through faith that we will see the goodness of the Lord, even in difficult circumstances.

- It is through faith in Jesus Christ that we will overcome the kingdom of darkness.

- It is through faith that we will continue to experience God's divine safety and protection in a fallen world.

## Faith Unlocks the Kingdom of God

Faith is not passive—it is the currency of the Kingdom. The more we trust in God, the greater our access to His divine realities.

*"We do not want you to become lazy, but to imitate those who through faith and patience inherit what has been promised."*
Hebrews 6:12[(NIV)]

Walking in the fullness of divine protection is not automatic—it requires faith and patience. Many have gone before us, standing firm in faith and obedience, and they have inherited the promises of God.

When we choose to live for Christ, we step into a new consciousness of divine safety and protection. This is not a mere theory—it is a supernatural reality made available through the finished work of Christ.

## Jesus Died to Give Us Abundant Life

We must never forget why Jesus came—not just for our salvation, but to give us life in abundance.

*"The thief comes only to steal and kill and destroy; I have come that they may have life, and have it to the full."* John 10:10[(NIV)]

Through His death and resurrection, Jesus provided:

- Forgiveness

- Justification

- Righteousness

- Eternal life

- Mercy and grace

- Peace

- Healing

- Divine safety and protection

As believers, we are called to live in the fullness of what Christ has made available to us. We do not merely exist—we thrive, protected under His mighty hand.

Our faith in God unlocks new dimensions of His Kingdom. When we walk in faith, we activate His supernatural safety and provision, ensuring that no weapon formed against us will prosper.

This is the reality of God's divine protection—a life fully surrendered, fully covered, and fully victorious in Christ. Hallelujah!

## Exercise Discernment and Wisdom.

The wisdom of God is a powerful shield, guiding us to make decisions that align with His will and protecting us from unnecessary dangers. Discernment enables us to identify potential threats, while wisdom helps us navigate life with divine insight.

*"For the Lord gives wisdom; from his mouth come knowledge and understanding. He holds success in store for the upright, he is a shield to those whose walk is blameless, for he guards the course of the just and protects the way of his faithful ones."*
Proverbs 2:6-8[NKJV]

Wisdom and discernment are gifts from God that act as a divine compass, ensuring we walk in His protection and favour. Those who seek wisdom gain insight into spiritual and physical dangers and are empowered to make choices that preserve and safeguard their lives.

## Live in Obedience to God

A life of obedience is a life of divine security. When we follow God's instructions, we position ourselves under His covering, ensuring that we walk in His protection, favour, and blessings.

*"If you fully obey the Lord your God and carefully follow all his commands I give you today, the Lord your God will set you high above all the nations on earth. All these blessings will come on you and accompany you if you obey the Lord your God."*
Deuteronomy 28:1-2(NIV)

Obedience is a gateway to God's supernatural provision, guidance, and protection. When we walk in alignment with His will, we experience His divine security in every area of our lives.

## Be Aware of God's Presence

Understanding that God is constantly with us is a source of comfort and assurance. His presence strengthens us, upholds us, and defends us in times of trouble.

*"God is our refuge and strength, an ever-present help in trouble."* Psalm 46:1(NIV)

No matter the circumstance, His presence remains unwavering. Whether we face physical, emotional, or spiritual battles, we can rest in the certainty that He is our divine protector and refuge.

## Cast Your Cares on Him

Carrying fear, anxiety, and worry can make us vulnerable to emotional, physical, and spiritual distress. The Lord calls us to surrender our burdens so that we can experience His peace, security, and rest.

> *"Cast all your anxiety on him because he cares for you."*
> 1 Peter 5:7[(NKJV)]

Letting go of our fears and uncertainties is an act of trusting in God's ability to safeguard us. He cares for us deeply and personally, ensuring that His divine protection surrounds us at all times.

## Walking in God's Divine Protection

By exercising discernment, walking in obedience, remaining aware of His presence, and surrendering our worries to Him, we position ourselves to experience God's supernatural safety and preservation.

God's protection is not just a concept—it is a tangible reality, accessible to all who trust, obey, and walk in faith. When we live in wisdom, obedience, and surrender, His hand of protection becomes undeniable and unshakable in our lives.

Hallelujah! We serve a God who watches over us, shields us, and keeps us safe in every season.

## Stay Connected to the Church

God never intended for us to walk this spiritual journey alone. Being part of a faith community strengthens us, offers support during trials, and helps us remain accountable in our walk with God.

*"And let us consider how we may spur one another on toward love and good deeds, not giving up meeting together, as some are in the habit of doing, but encouraging one another—and all the more as you see the Day approaching."* Hebrews 10:24-25[NKJV]

A church community provides spiritual covering, encouragement, and a place where believers can pray for one another, learn, and grow together. It fosters a sense of belonging and ensures that we are not isolated and vulnerable to the attacks of the enemy.

## Offer Praise and Thanksgiving

One of the most powerful weapons in a believer's life is praise and thanksgiving. When we cultivate a heart of gratitude, we remain focused on God's faithfulness and goodness, rather than our fears and troubles.

> *"Enter his gates with thanksgiving and his courts with praise; give thanks to him and praise his name."* Psalm 100:4[NIV]

Thanksgiving shifts our perspective and strengthens our faith, enabling us to trust in God's unwavering protection. When we praise God, we invite His presence into our circumstances, and His presence is a place of security and refuge.

## Pray for Protection

Prayer is our direct line of communication with God. It is the key to receiving divine safety, peace, and wisdom. Through prayer, we bring our concerns, fears, and needs before God, trusting Him to guide, protect, and preserve us.

> *"Do not be anxious about anything, but in every situation, by prayer and petition, with thanksgiving, present your requests to God. And the peace of God, which transcends all understanding, will guard your hearts and your minds in Christ Jesus."*
> Philippians 4:6-7[NKJV]

Instead of allowing anxiety and fear to rule our hearts, we are encouraged to bring everything to God in prayer. In return, He grants us peace, which serves as a protective shield over our hearts and minds.

## Living in the Reality of God's Protection

By staying connected to the church, cultivating a heart of thanksgiving, and making prayer a daily practice, we position ourselves under God's divine protection.

His promises are eternal, His presence unwavering, and His shield impenetrable. Those who seek Him, trust Him, and walk in His ways will continually experience His supernatural safety and security in every aspect of life.

Hallelujah! God is our fortress, our refuge, and our protector, now and forevermore!

# Spiritual Warfare: Battle Ready!

**Heavenly Father,**

I come before You today, seeking Your divine protection and strength. As I prepare to face the challenges of this world, I clothe myself in the full Armour of God, as described in Ephesians 6:10-18.

### The Belt of Truth

Lord, help me to stand firm with the belt of truth buckled around my waist. Let Your truth guide my thoughts and actions, keeping me honest, steadfast, and unwavering in all I do.

*"Then you will know the truth, and the truth will set you free."*
*John 8:32*(NIV)

### The Breastplate of Righteousness

*I put on the breastplate of righteousness, protecting my heart from the temptations, corruption, and evil of this world. Help me to live a life that reflects Your righteousness, making me a light in the darkness.*

*"Above all else, guard your heart, for everything you do flows from it." Proverbs 4:23*(NKJV)

### The Gospel of Peace

I fit my feet with the readiness that comes from the gospel of peace. May I walk in Your peace, standing firm even in storms and trials, spreading Your love, grace, and tranquillity wherever I go.

*"And the peace of God, which transcends all understanding, will guard your hearts and your minds in Christ Jesus." Philippians 4:7*(NKJV)

### The Shield of Faith

I take up the shield of faith, with which I extinguish all the flaming arrows of the evil one. Strengthen my faith, Lord, that I may trust You without doubt, hesitation, or fear.

*"Now faith is confidence in what we hope for and assurance about what we do not see." Hebrews 11:1*(NKJV)

### The Helmet of Salvation

I put on the helmet of salvation, guarding my mind, thoughts, and spirit from the lies of the enemy. Let the assurance of my salvation be my strength and confidence. Remind me, Lord, that I am Yours, redeemed and victorious through Christ.

*"But since we belong to the day, let us be sober, putting on faith and love as a breastplate, and the hope of salvation as a helmet." 1 Thessalonians 5:8*(NKJV)

### The Sword of the Spirit

I take up the sword of the Spirit, which is Your Word, the ultimate weapon of truth, power, and authority against every attack of the enemy. Let Your Word be alive in me, cutting through lies, deception, and darkness.

*"For the word of God is alive and active. Sharper than any double-edged sword, it penetrates even to dividing soul and spirit, joints and marrow; it judges the thoughts and attitudes of the heart." Hebrews 4:12*(NKJV)

### Praying in the Spirit

Finally, I commit to praying in the Spirit on all occasions, lifting my requests to You, standing in faith and persistence, and remaining vigilant and alert in my prayers for all believers.

*"Pray continually." 1 Thessalonians 5:17*

Lord, with Your Armour, I am battle-ready. I stand secure, bold, and victorious, knowing that You fight for me. Thank You for Your divine protection, strength, and unfailing guidance.

In the mighty name of Jesus, Amen!

**22**

# ENGAGING THE SUPERNATURAL

The Power of Prophetic Declarations

---

Spiritual engagement through prophetic declarations is a vital practice for every believer seeking to align their life with God's promises. In this chapter, we explore how speaking God's Word activates supernatural realities, strengthens faith, and brings divine protection into our lives. Through prayer and intercession, we not only position ourselves under His covering but also stand in the gap for the vulnerable—orphans, widows, and the homeless. As we declare, believe, and intercede, we partner with Heaven to see God's power manifest in our lives and in the lives of those in need.

Prophetic declarations are a powerful way of verbalising our faith in God, aligning our hearts and minds with His Word and promises. By daily declaring scripture and prophetic confessions, we actively engage in the supernatural realm, reinforcing our trust in God's divine protection against the enemy, challenging circumstances, and the uncertainties of this fallen world.

If you have not yet read the Preface of this book, I strongly encourage you to start there first. It will provide a solid foundation for understanding the significance and power of what we are about to embark upon. I believe that as you do so, you will be greatly blessed and spiritually strengthened.

## The Power of Prophetic Declarations

Declaring God's Word has a transformative impact on our spiritual atmosphere, mindset, and faith. When we declare scripture, we are not merely speaking words—we are activating the supernatural, commanding our circumstances to align with God's promises, and standing in agreement with Heaven.

One of the remarkable things I have noticed while making prophetic declarations is that they ignite a deeper passion for prayer. As I declare, I often find myself interceding for situations I never initially intended to pray for. This divine leading of the Holy Spirit expands our spiritual capacity and draws us into deeper communion with God.

Are you ready to activate your faith and experience the miraculous?

## A Call to Intercession

As we engage our faith in prayer, let us take a moment to lift up those who are vulnerable in our society. Let us pray for:

- Orphans, that they may experience the love of the Heavenly Father and be cared for in a safe and nurturing environment.

- Widows, that God may comfort, provide, and strengthen them in their times of need.

- The homeless, that they may receive shelter, provision, and restoration, experiencing the compassion and kindness of God's people.

### Isaiah 1:17(NKJV)
*"Learn to do right; seek justice. Defend the oppressed. Take up the cause of the fatherless; plead the case of the widow."*

As we stand in faith and declare God's Word over our lives, let us also intercede for others, believing that God's protection, provision, and mercy will extend to all who are in need.

Let us pray, declare, and stand firm in the knowledge that God's Word never returns void (Isaiah 55:11). The supernatural is real, and as we engage spiritually, we will see the manifestation of God's power in our lives and in the lives of others.

Are you ready? Let us declare and engage in faith!

## A Prayer for Orphans, Widows, and the Homeless

Heavenly Father,

I come before You with a heart full of compassion for the orphans, widows, and homeless individuals in South Africa and across the world. I lift them up before You, knowing that You are a Father to the fatherless, a defender of widows, and a shelter for the homeless (Psalm 68:5).

Lord, we ask for Your divine protection over these vulnerable individuals. Surround them with Your angels, keeping them safe from all harm (Psalm 91:11). Shield them from danger, abuse, neglect, and any form of injustice. Let no weapon formed against them prosper (Isaiah 54:17).

Father, I pray for their spiritual well-being. Guard their hearts and minds in Christ Jesus (Philippians 4:7). May they come to know You as their Saviour, finding comfort, peace, and purpose in Your presence. Fill them with Your Holy Spirit, guiding them in all truth and righteousness (John 16:13).

I declare that these orphans, widows, and homeless individuals will experience Your love and provision through the people You place in their lives. May they never feel abandoned or alone, for You have promised never to leave nor forsake them (Hebrews 13:5).

I proclaim that they will find refuge and strength in You, their ever-present help in times of trouble (Psalm 46:1). I speak life and hope over their futures, believing that You will restore what has been lost and bring beauty from ashes (Isaiah 61:3).

*"The Lord is my shepherd; I shall not want. He makes me lie down in green pastures. He leads me beside still waters. He restores my soul"* (Psalm 23:1-3[NKJV])

May they find rest, restoration, and peace in You.

*"For I know the plans I have for you, declares the Lord, plans for welfare and not for evil, to give you a future and a hope"* (Jeremiah 29:11[NKJV]). Lord, we trust in Your good and perfect plans for their lives.

*"He will cover you with his feathers, and under his wings, you will find refuge; his faithfulness will be your shield and rampart"* (Psalm 91:4[NKJV]). May they find safety, security, and comfort under Your wings.

Lord, I thank You for hearing my prayer and for Your unfailing love, protection, and provision over these orphans, widows, and homeless individuals. May they grow in wisdom, stature, and favour with both God and man (Luke 2:52).

In Jesus' mighty name, I pray. Amen.

## 23

# DECLARING VICTORY

Daily Prophetic Declarations for Divine Protection

---

The words we speak have power—power to shape our reality, align our lives with God's promises, and activate His divine protection. Scripture teaches that life and death are in the power of the tongue (Proverbs 18:21). When we declare God's Word over our lives, we invite His supernatural covering, favour, and provision into our daily walk.

This chapter provides a set of daily prophetic declarations, rooted in Scripture, designed to equip you for victory, strengthen your faith, and fortify your spirit. As you boldly speak these truths, expect to see breakthroughs, divine protection, and the tangible presence of God manifesting in your life. Let us step into each day with confidence, declaring God's promises and walking in His unshakable covering!

As believers, the power of spoken declarations cannot be underestimated. When we declare God's Word over our lives, we align ourselves with His promises and activate His divine protection, favour, and provision. Scripture teaches us that life and death are in the power of the tongue (Proverbs 18:21), meaning that our words carry spiritual authority.

Each day presents new challenges and opportunities, but through prayer, faith, and prophetic declarations, we position ourselves under the covering of God's divine presence. By confessing His Word daily, we fortify our spirits, renew our minds, and establish His truth over our circumstances.

The following daily declarations are designed to help you speak God's promises over your life, your family, and your future. As you boldly proclaim these truths, expect to see supernatural breakthroughs, divine protection, and the tangible presence of God in every area of your life.

Now, let us step into a week of victory, breakthrough, and divine safety as we decree and declare God's Word over each day!

# Monday

Psalm 34:7[(NKJV)]
*"The angel of the LORD encamps around those who fear him,
and he delivers them. "*

### DECLARATION

Thank You, Lord, that I am protected, and that Your angel encamps around me and my family. Because of Your divine covering, no weapon formed against us shall prosper. Your mighty hand of safety delivers us from every scheme and attack of the enemy.

We are covered, sealed, and preserved for purpose, set apart to experience Your goodness in the land of the living. Today, I decree and declare the blood of Jesus over my life, my family, and everything that concerns us. I render the works of darkness null and void, cancelling every accident, attack, and incident orchestrated by the kingdom of darkness against us.

Every trap set by the enemy is exposed and will not prevail. I decree and declare that we will live and not die before our time. What was meant for our demise will be turned around for our good.

Today, we walk in blessing, divine favour, and victory. The grace of the Lord will be evident in all we do, empowering us to overcome every challenge and remain victorious in all areas of life.

I declare that I am blessed and highly favoured of the Lord. I command every good and perfect gift from God to find me today. In Jesus' mighty name, Amen!

# Tuesday

### Deuteronomy 31:6(NIV)

*"Be strong and courageous. Do not be afraid or terrified because of them, for the Lord your God goes with you; He will never leave you nor forsake you."*

### DECLARATION:

I decree and declare, in the mighty name of Jesus, that I will be strong and courageous in God. I refuse to be afraid or terrified—whether by circumstances, sickness, crime, spiritual or physical threats, rejection, or lack. For my God goes before me today, leveling mountains, making the crooked places straight, and providing rivers of water in dry and desolate places.

I reject every lie from the kingdom of darkness that tries to convince me that I am alone. The Word of God assures me that I am never alone, for He is always with me and for me. Therefore, today will be a day of joy, peace, contentment, and victory. Strength and courage are my portion!

I declare that I am covered, for the Lord is my refuge and my strength in times of trouble. I am above and not beneath, victorious and not a victim. Thank You, Holy Spirit, for dwelling within me now and forevermore. I stand firm in faith, knowing that no weapon formed against me shall prosper, in Jesus' mighty name, Amen!

# Wednesday

**Psalm 121:7-8**[NIV]

*"The Lord will keep you from all harm—He will watch over your life; the Lord will watch over your coming and going both now and forevermore."*

## DECLARATION

Oh, wonderful Father of grace, mercy, lovingkindness, and peace, I thank You for this powerful reminder that You will keep me from all harm. Therefore, I boldly decree and declare that You, my God, will watch over my life, my children, my spouse, my grandchildren, and all my family members in the name of Jesus. I declare that You will watch over our coming and going, both now and forevermore.

In the mighty name of Jesus, I cancel and destroy every form of harm plotted against us. Whether at work, school, the shops, or anywhere we go, You, my wonderful Saviour, will watch over us. Your grace and mercy will overtake us. Whether we are on the road, rail, sea, air, or simply walking, we will be protected and preserved, for we are sealed in Christ through the Holy Spirit.

I declare that this day is blessed and will align with heaven's purpose for my life. In the name of Jesus, I bind and rebuke every evil weapon formed against me, my family, and my destiny. According to Job 5:19-26, I decree and declare that no enchantment, divination, or bewitchment against my life and destiny shall succeed!

Heavenly Father, as Psalm 35:1 & 4 declares, contend with those who contend with me; fight against those who fight against me. May those who seek my life be disgraced and put to shame; may those who plot my ruin be turned back in dismay.

I speak the blood of Jesus Christ over my family, my community, our country, our governmental leaders, and our spiritual leaders. I cover every pastor, evangelist, prophet, teacher, and apostle in the precious blood of Jesus Christ. Lord, grant them more grace and strength to carry out Your divine will for their lives.

In Jesus' mighty name, I pray and declare, Amen!

# Thursday

Psalm 32:7<sup>(NIV)</sup>

*"You are my hiding place; You will protect me from trouble and surround me with songs of deliverance."*

## DECLARATION

Thank You, Lord, that You are my hiding place. Because of this truth, I boldly declare that I am protected from trouble and that You will surround me with songs of deliverance. I will continue to witness Your goodness and mercy all the days of my life. What a powerful scripture, reassuring me that my God is with me and for me!

Father, hide me from every attack of the enemy. Hide me from depression, from financial struggles, from sickness, from evil arrows, and from those who seek to destroy me. Hide my children, my spouse, my business, my career, and my ministry. Hide everything that concerns me under Your mighty wings. In Your hiding place, I will be surrounded with songs of deliverance, witnessing Your mighty hand of rescue in times of trouble.

I will make a joyful noise to the Lord, because I know that His divine protection covers me. I decree and declare that God's hiding protection will shield me from all harm—whether at work, in my business, in my ministry, in my marriage, in my finances, and in my health.

Lord, hide our country and our communities from terrorism, violence, genocide, and racial discrimination. I declare the blood of Jesus over South Africa, covering our land, our people, and our future. I speak divine protection over the homeless, the orphans, and the widows. Father, be their hiding place today, shielding them from trouble and commanding Your angels to watch over them.

I declare and decree that every child who has been abducted from their home and family will be rescued! You, my God, will cover them and protect them. I plead the blood of Jesus over every missing child. I rebuke and bind every evil force behind this wickedness. Let Your Holy Spirit arrest those responsible, in the mighty name of Jesus Christ.

Be their hiding place, Lord! Be their deliverance! Let the oppressed go free! In Jesus' name, I pray and declare, Amen!

# Friday

## Romans 8:31[(NKJV)]

"What, then, shall we say in response to these things? If God is for us, who can be against us?"

## DECLARATION

I decree and declare—what a mighty God we serve! The King of Kings and Lord of Lords—who can stand against Him? No one! Because He is for me, no devil in hell can prevail against me. No force of disappointment, discouragement, or hopelessness will succeed in its mission to break me, because greater is He who is in me than he who is in the world (1 John 4:4).

No wizard, no witchdoctor, no scheme of darkness, nor any force in all creation that has been designed to bring me harm shall stand, because my God—my God!—the One who upholds all creation by His word, is with me and for me (Hebrews 1:3).

Father, according to Psalm 27:12, do not deliver me over to the will of my enemies. I declare and decree that the spirit of power, love, and a sound mind is at work in me, surrounding and guiding me. Today will be no different from all the wonderful, peaceful, productive, and blessed days that I have walked with You, my Lord. Since I am fully aware of the indisputable fact that Yahweh Nissi—the Lord my Banner, my Refuge—is with me, I will fear no evil, for I am protected, covered, loved, and accepted!

Who can be against me if the Creator of heaven and earth is for me and with me? I refuse to walk timidly because of my adversaries! I stand boldly in the confidence of Christ, for Jehovah Elohim (Mighty One) and Jehovah El Shaddai (The All-Sufficient One) are with me!

I declare today blessed! Every blessing that has my name on it will find its way to me without hindrance in the name of Jesus! I rebuke every satanic delay and every form of sabotage against my breakthrough, my blessings, my peace, and my joy in the name of Jesus!

This is the day that the Lord has made—I will rejoice and be glad in it! Hallelujah!

# Saturday

### Psalm 27:1-5<sup>(NKJV)</sup>

*"The Lord is my light and my salvation—whom shall I fear? The Lord is the stronghold of my life—of whom shall I be afraid? When the wicked advance against me to devour me, it is my enemies and my foes who will stumble and fall. Though an army besiege me, my heart will not fear; though war break out against me, even then I will be confident. One thing I ask from the Lord, this only do I seek: that I may dwell in the house of the Lord all the days of my life, to gaze on the beauty of the Lord and to seek Him in His temple. For in the day of trouble He will keep me safe in His dwelling; He will hide me in the shelter of His sacred tent and set me high upon a rock."*

### DECLARATION

I declare and decree—the Lord is my light and my salvation! Whom shall I fear? No one and nothing! The Lord is the stronghold of my life, and because of this unshakable truth, fear has no hold on me! Every wicked scheme, every enemy that rises against me will stumble and fall, for the power of God surrounds me.

Even if an army besieges me, my heart will not fear. Even if war breaks out against me, I will stand firm and confident in my Lord.

My confidence is in Christ alone, for He is my refuge, my strong tower, and my fortress in times of trouble.

Lord, I desire nothing more than to dwell in Your presence all the days of my life. I long to gaze upon Your beauty, to be anchored in Your presence, and to seek You in Your holy temple. For in the day of trouble, You will keep me safe! You will hide me under the shadow of Your wings. You will set me high upon a rock, far beyond the reach of danger.

Because You are my light, I will walk in clarity. Because You are my salvation, I will walk in hope. Because You are my stronghold, I will walk in victory. Your divine safety, protection, and deliverance are mine, and no force in hell can remove me from Your covering.

Darkness is dispelled! Fear is eradicated! Every attack of the enemy is cancelled! The light of Christ shines upon me, guiding my steps in peace, favour, and victory! In Jesus' mighty name, Amen!

# Sunday

### Psalm 91:1-16 [NKJV]

*"Whoever dwells in the shelter of the Most High will rest in the shadow of the Almighty. I will say of the Lord, 'He is my refuge and my fortress, my God, in whom I trust.' Surely, he will save you from the fowler's snare and from the deadly pestilence. He will cover you with his feathers, and under his wings you will find refuge; his faithfulness will be your shield and rampart. You will not fear the terror of night, nor the arrow that flies by day, nor the pestilence that stalks in the darkness, nor the plague that destroys at midday. A thousand may fall at your side, ten thousand at your right hand, but it will not come near you. You will only observe with your eyes and see the punishment of the wicked. If you say, 'The Lord is my refuge,' and you make the Most High your dwelling, no harm will overtake you, no disaster will come near your tent. For he will command his angels concerning you to guard you in all your ways; they will lift you up in their hands, so that you will not strike your foot against a stone. You will tread on the lion and the cobra; you will trample the great lion and the serpent. 'Because he loves me,' says the Lord, 'I will rescue him; I will protect him, for he acknowledges my name. He will call on me, and I will answer him; I will be with him in trouble, I will deliver him and honour him. With long life I will satisfy him and show him my salvation.'"*

## DECLARATION

I declare and decree that I dwell in the shelter of the Most High, and I rest in the shadow of the Almighty. The Lord is my refuge, my fortress, my shield, and my ever-present help in times of trouble. No weapon formed against me shall prosper, and no harm shall come near my dwelling.

Every plan of the enemy is dismantled! Every trap set before me is exposed and destroyed! The arrows that fly by day shall not find me; the terror that prowls at night shall not afflict me. Every plague, sickness, and disaster shall pass over me, for I am marked by the blood of Jesus Christ!

I call upon the name of the Lord, and He answers me! He rescues me, protects me, and surrounds me with His angels. I am victorious! I walk in divine protection, strength, favour, and peace. I trample over every attack of the serpent and scorpion—Satan and all his schemes have no hold on me! The fire of God surrounds me, and His glory is my covering!

As I step into this new week, I partner with heaven in prayer. I intercede for my family, my community, and my nation. I declare breakthroughs, healing, deliverance, and divine intervention over every area of my life. The atmosphere is shifting! God is working behind the scenes on my behalf!

Today, I stand boldly in faith. My testimony is secured, my destiny is aligned, and my spirit is strengthened in the Lord. So shall it be in the mighty name of Jesus Christ!

## 24

# A NEW BEGINNING

Embracing Salvation in Christ

---

Salvation is the greatest gift ever given—an invitation into eternal life, divine protection, and unshakable fellowship with God. If you have been reading this book and feel a stirring in your heart, know that it is not by chance. God has been calling you into His loving arms, offering you a new beginning.

This chapter presents an opportunity to surrender your life to Jesus Christ and step into His grace, mercy, and divine covering. As you pray the Sinner's Prayer, may you experience the joy of salvation, the peace of His presence, and the assurance that you are now part of God's eternal family. Heaven rejoices over you today!

## Sinners' Prayer

If you have been reading this book and have yet to accept the Lord Jesus Christ as your personal Saviour, I want to extend this opportunity to you. The mere fact that you have reached the end of this book is a clear sign that God has been speaking to you, drawing you closer to His divine love and protection. I encourage you to take this life-changing step and pray this prayer with me:

# Prayer

*Dear Heavenly Father,*

*I come before You today in the name of Jesus Christ, acknowledging that I am a sinner in need of Your grace and salvation. Thank You for the gift of life, for Your divine mercy, and for allowing me to complete this book on divine safety and protection. I recognise that I cannot save myself, and I humbly ask for Your forgiveness.*

*Lord, please cleanse me, wash me, and purify me with the precious blood of Jesus Christ. I renounce the devil and his kingdom, and I completely surrender my life to You today. Come into my heart, Lord Jesus, and take Your rightful place as my Lord and Saviour.*

*Your Word declares in Romans 10:10 that if I believe in my heart and confess with my mouth that Jesus died and rose again, I will be saved. Today, I wholeheartedly believe in my heart and confess with my mouth that Jesus Christ is Lord and that He was raised from the dead. I declare and decree that from this moment forward, I am born again, a new creation in Christ!*

*Thank You, Lord, for saving me! Thank You for writing my name in the Book of Life! I now belong to You, and I will live for You all the days of my life. In Jesus' mighty name, Amen!*

---

**Welcome to the Family of God!**

If you have prayed this prayer, congratulations!

You have made the most important decision of your life. The Bible tells us in Luke 15:10 that *there is great rejoicing in heaven over one sinner who repents.* Right now, all of heaven is celebrating your new life in Christ!

To grow in your faith, I encourage you to find a Word-based, Spirit-filled local church where you can fellowship, serve, and be strengthened in your walk with God. Surround yourself with like-minded believers who will support and encourage you on this journey.

May the Lord bless you, keep you, and guide you as you embark on this new chapter of walking in His divine protection, grace, and love. You are no longer the same—welcome to the family of God!

## COVERED FOR LIFE

As this journey comes to a close, remember this: divine protection is not just a biblical concept. It is your covenant reality. Through every declaration, prayer, and promise in these pages, God has been equipping you to walk boldly and live fearlessly. You have been called to live covered—not occasionally, but continually.

Don't shrink back. Rise up. Keep speaking. Keep believing. Keep walking.

You are covered. You are protected. You are never alone.

Yahweh Nissi is your banner—and His banner over you is love.

# REFERENCE INDEX

1. *Mbambo, N. (2015). Jehovah Is Your Name [Song]. Spirit and Life (Live). Koko Records.*
2. Smallwood, L. (2013) The God Behind the Names [Revision of "The Name & Attributes of God"]. Available at: https://myredeemerlives.com (Accessed: 13 January 2024).
3. World English Bible (n.d.) Available at: https://worldenglish.bible (Accessed: 13 January 2024).
4. South African Police Service (2019) Annual Crime Report. Available at: https://www.saps.gov.za/about/stratframework/annual_report/2019_2020/annual_crime_report_2019_2020.pdf (Accessed: 28 November 2023).
5. Bible Hub (2021) Strong's Greek: 2198. ζάω (zaó) -- To live, to be alive. Available at: https://biblehub.com/greek/2198.htm (Accessed: 18 April 2024).

6. Bible Hub (2021) Strong's Greek: 1411. δύναμις (dunamis) -- Power, strength, ability, might, miracle. Available at: https://biblehub.com/greek/1411.htm (Accessed: 18 April 2024).

7. Pulpit Commentary (n.d.) Available at: https://biblehub.com/commentaries/job/22-28.htm (Accessed: 18 April 2024).

8. Matthew Pool Commentary (n.d.) Available at: https://biblehub.com/commentaries/job/22-28.htm (Accessed: 18 April 2024).

9. Ibiyeomie, D. (2013) Understanding Divine Protection. Salvation Ministries.

10. Chabad (2025) Understanding the Soul in Hebrew Scriptures. Available at: https://www.chabad.org (Accessed: 18 February 2025).

11. Parsons, J. J. (2023) Hebrew for Christians. Available at: https://hebrew4christians.com/About_HFC/about_hfc.html (Accessed: 9 January 2024).

12. Wilson, R. F. (2023) God Our Refuge and Fortress. Available at: https://www.jesuswalk.com (Accessed: 18 January 2024).

13. Bible Hub (n.d.) Hebrew: māgēn. Available at: https://biblehub.com/hebrew/4043.htm (Accessed: 18 April 2025).

14. Strong's Concordance (n.d.) Greek: agapao. Available at: https://biblehub.com/greek/25.htm (Accessed: 18 April 2025).

15. Bible Hub (n.d.) Greek: ἄγγελος (Angelos). Available at: https://biblehub.com/greek/32.htm (Accessed: 18 April 2025).

16. Bennett, B. (2017) Effectual, fervent prayer. Barry Bennett Ministries. (p. 15) (Accessed: 18 January 2024).

17. Collins, M. G. (1997) The Sixth Commandment. Bibletools.org. Available at: https://bibletools.org (Accessed: 27 December 2023).

18. Bible Hub (2021) Strong's Greek: 4991. σωτηρία (sótéria) -- Salvation. Available at: https://biblehub.com/greek/4991.htm (Accessed: 27 December 2023).

19. Robinson, L., Smith, M., & Segal, J. (2023) Understanding emotional and psychological trauma. HelpGuide. (p. 45) (Accessed: 18 January 2024).

20. Renner, R. (n.d.) Another Comforter. Renner Ministries. Available at: https://renner.org/article/another-comforter/#:~:text=%E2%80%94%20John%2014:16&text=He%20said%2C%20%E2%80%9CI%20will%20pray,of%20the%20very%20same%20kind (Accessed: 20 April 2025).

www.ingramcontent.com/pod-product-compliance
Lightning Source LLC
Chambersburg PA
CBHW021141090426
42740CB00008B/874